1 MONTH OF
FREE
READING

at

www.ForgottenBooks.com

By purchasing this book you are eligible for one month membership to ForgottenBooks.com, giving you unlimited access to our entire collection of over 1,000,000 titles via our web site and mobile apps.

To claim your free month visit:

www.forgottenbooks.com/free821468

ISBN 978-0-365-28619-6
PIBN 10821468

Forgotten Books is a registered trademark of FB &c Ltd.
Copyright © 2018 FB &c Ltd.
FB &c Ltd, Dalton House, 60 Windsor Avenue, London, SW19 2RR.
Company number 08720141. Registered in England and Wales.

For support please visit www.forgottenbooks.com

COMEDIES AND LEGENDS FOR MARIONETTES

A Theatre for Boys and Girls

BY

GEORGIANA GODDARD KING

ILLUSTRATED BY ANNA R. GILES

New York

THE MACMILLAN COMPANY

LONDON: MACMILLAN & CO., Ltd.

1904

Norwood Press
J. S. Cushing & Co. — Berwick & Smith Co.
Norwood, Mass., U.S.A.

CONTENTS

COMEDIES

LEGENDS

PANTOMIMES

ILLUSTRATIONS

TO MAKE A MARIONETTE THEATRE

LONG ago, when people gave me toy theatres in which the actors were paper dolls, or mere silhouettes for shadow comedies, I always threw away the accompanying printed plays because I found them dull and silly. The plays I made up in their stead were much like those in this volume. Other themes will occur to any one who has made himself a set of marionettes, or he may adapt, for his playhouse, dramas already written — the tragical comedy of Pyramus and Thisbe out of Shakespeare, or produce, as I once did for a parish school feast, the miracle play from Longfellow's *Golden Legend.*

So far as I know, it is not possible to get in this country a full set of toy marionettes. For these are, after all, only simulacra, shadows of a theatre for grown men and women with puppets four or five

To Make a Marionette Theatre

feet high. Nay more, there is a theatre at which living actors pretend to be marionettes, mimicking the stiff motions, the ungainly sorrows and fantastic mirth of the painted wooden creatures. But that does not concern us.

A clever boy or girl can easily make the puppets or can use ordinary dolls rather loose in the arm and thigh joints. In the latter case the dolls should have a stout wire around the waist under the clothes, running up the back, secured at the neck by another ring of wire (easily concealed under a ruff or a necklace), thence going up back of the head for several inches, bent at the end into a hook. A slender wire or a thread with a ring attached is fastened to the right wrist, or, if the marionettes are large, there is one for each arm, which controls the movements of the arm. Thus the little actors can walk and run, sit down and rise again, shake hands, fight, or embrace, in short, do enough to keep the stage in constant activity.

If you undertake to make them, you need only a doll for model, wire of different sizes, tiny wire staples, soft pine, a knife, sandpaper, and a few paints. Whittle out the hand and forearm in one piece, and the leg, ending in a boot or a slipper, the trunk, the

To Make a Marionette Theatre

head and neck, with nose and eye-sockets somewhat shaped. After these are carefully sandpapered, paint them with ordinary oil paints or even with water-colours, first covering them, in that case, thickly and smoothly with Chinese white. Drive a tiny staple into the end of the arm, loop one end of a bit of wire into it and the other end into a similar staple driven into the side of the trunk at the shoulder. Attach the other arm in the same way; the legs, similarly, to the bottom of the trunk, and these are not jointed at the knees. The head, which has the large wire firmly embedded in it, is fastened at the neck rather loosely to the body, so that it can turn from side to side. Now the puppet must be dressed like a doll in coat and trousers or petticoat, these being sewed on. There are, of course, no underclothes, and cheap, gay calicoes and cottony satins are best, because they are what the real Italian marionettes wear. Certain characters — harlequin, the clown, the captain, the merchant — are always the same whatever the play.

Properties—the lute, the sword, etc.—are made of wood, paper, or tin, and painted. The swords and shields should be of tin for the noise; the latter round, hung on the left wrist by a loop, the former

To Make a Marionette Theatre

with a long, slim blade thrust through a hole in the
puppet's fist.   Lighter objects may be stuck to the
hand with cobbler's wax.

The size of the theatre depends on the size of
the puppets; the arch should be not quite twice as
high as they. Find a shallow wooden box, take out
the lid and one side, or knock out one side of a
strawberry crate and set it up on the long, narrow
edge.   There you have the open front toward your
audience, and through the top you operate the actors.
It is well to stretch a couple of stout wires or thin
rods across this top and bend the ends of the puppet
wires so that when these are hooked over the rods
the feet of the puppets will just touch the floor.
Then a character who is on the scene but not active
may be hung in his place and leave your hands free
to operate those who are talking.   Cut a piece of
pasteboard the size and shape of the whole front,
draw in a low, wide curve the outline of the proscenium arch with straight sides, leaving a few inches
up the sides and at the top of the arch.   Paint this
to imitate the similar arch in a real theatre.   Then
cut it out and glue it to the front. You may hang
a little red curtain in the curve of the arch if you
find your hands showing. The scenery, painted on

To Make a Marionette Theatre

pasteboard or paper, is fastened to the back, and the characters move right and left in front of it: there is only one pair of "wings" on each side; that is, straight pieces running up and down between which the characters enter and go out, painted like the little curtain that hangs from the arch. Or if you wish to be very elaborate, make separate sets for indoors, street, and the wood or garden — painted respectively with wall and curtains, part of the front of a house, and green trees or bushes. I have found broad, flat water-colour work the best, though I have sometimes used oil paints: and the buildings, garden, etc., may be copies from a picture. For the play of *The Magic Hat* the scenery would be somewhat as follows: —

Scene I, the façade of a great church going up out of sight. The main lines of this may be got from a picture of a Continental cathedral. Scene II, a garden — say a wall with hollyhocks growing up against it and treetops above. If the piece is to be very elaborate, set at the left a similar wall, joining it at the back at a very obtuse angle about one-third from the end. In this is a gate of iron bars cut out so that Leander shows when he stands behind it; if it is hinged with thin, tough paper, he can

To Make a Marionette Theatre

push it open. Out on the stage is set a flat, cut-out piece for the arbour or thicket, with a flat foot like the trees of a toy village. Scene III, the wall of a room with pictures on it, or the corner showing a part of the floor in violent perspective.

Rig a little curtain that rolls, or runs with tiny rings on a wire strung across the back of the proscenium. Set the theatre on a table and set the table in a doorway, dropping a curtain to touch the top of the proscenium. Rehearse — or if alone, enact — your plays in front of a mirror : then you are manager and audience at once.

I have spoken as if there were but one operator, but there should be at least two — a boy and a girl for choice — to manipulate the three or four puppets on the stage simultaneously and to speak respectively the men's and the women's parts.

The puppets are laid out ready on the back of the table behind the theatre; lift one by the wire, slip the ring over your forefinger, plump him down on the stage at the left where the wings hide him, then move him toward your right into view. If he is big enough and loose enough, you can make him go one step at a time. Lift your forefinger and he lifts his arm. Remember that every speech has its appropriate gesture; in that lies the secret of the marionette drama. The rest is practice.

The many songs in the plays may quite well be spoken, if the *impresario* is not a singer; but even then I would suggest having some one at the piano on the occasion of a public performance, to take the part which the orchestra fills in the ordinary theatre: the songs will most of them go to familiar airs.

COMEDIES

THE LOYAL TWO

PUPPETS

MERCHANT, *Mira's father.*	Red suit, sword in hand.
ROGER } *twin brothers,* MILES } *gentlemen adventurers.*	Court dress, sword in hand.
TONY } *rogues and robbers.* TOBY }	Harlequins, with swords in their hands and shields on their arms.
CLOWN, *the Merchant's servant.*	
MIRA, *the Merchant's daughter.*	Court dress.
MARIAN, *his other daughter, stolen when a child.*	Peasant dress.
FAN, *waiting woman.*	Short dress, cap.
A servant of the Merchant's.	Clown's dress.
A number of robbers.	In green, with masks, round shields, and swords.

Properties : a gold chain, a lute.

The Loyal Two

ACT I

SCENE: *A Wood.*

Enter, L., MERCHANT, *who looks about, followed by* CLOWN *and* SERVANT, *who do the same.*

Clown. This is where we were, master, this morning at nine o' the sun, for in this wood a man may not even ask what's o'clock.

Servant. I recognize that twisted root like a grinning face.

Clown. And I that gaping face, much like a donkey preparing to bray. [*Strikes him.*]

23

Merchant. Peace, peace! Have I travelled over the wide world only to perish miserably close to my own home?

Clown. Cheer up, master; dying is no more than dying, here or on the deep sea; and for my part commend me to a dry end.

Servant. If master would have hired a guide, now, we should be home to dinner.

Clown. And now it is the wild beasts that will be home to dinner. They will find us here all ready.

Merchant. Surely this wood is bewitched; for, if I am not wrong, it was hereabout that my little child Marian was lost long years ago. I will struggle no more, but let the wolves and bears, which doubtless devoured her, feed upon me in turn.

Clown. I have no such regard for posterity as to let the grandchildren of them that ate the daughter dine off the father. Up, sir; let us try this path.

Merchant. I will not stir, to be again misled.

Clown. He that won't walk for fear of going wrong may stay where he is till he sprouts roots and leaves. Then will we go home alone, if not by one path, so by another.   [*Exeunt* CLOWN *and* SERVANT, *R.*

Merchant. The grief for my one child comes fresh upon me when I think that the other must

" I will struggle no more."

so soon be left alone in the world. What is that moving yonder?

Enter Tony *and* Toby. *They fight with him; he beats off one but is defeated by the other.*

Tony. You are our prisoner.

Merchant. I yield myself.

Toby. Kindly yield your purse. [*Exit* Merchant, *L.*] I know this gentleman. He lives not far, and has the fairest and most excellent daughter in the world.

Tony. Then instead of his being our prisoner why should not one of us be his son-in-law?

Toby. The thought was mine already, but we will not quarrel; when we have her we will toss a penny to determine the bridegroom. But how to get her?

Tony. He would sooner accept the blind beggar at the town gate.

Toby. Did I not say she was as dutiful as beautiful? I have it. This way, sir.

Enter Merchant, *L.*

Merchant. Rascals, I am in your power, but do not hope for a ransom. I am not a rich man.

Toby. Oh, good sir, you mistake us; we are not greedy, we are only poor fellows that would live, and must live in the world; if in the world, then by the world.

Tony. Which is to say, on the world.

Toby. And so bid the world go by.

Tony. Your purse, sir, will keep us from want this coming winter, and we will set you on the straight road for home with the best will in the world.

Toby. As we bear you no malice, so we would gladly know that you are well disposed toward us.

Merchant. Truly I cannot be rude to such kindly rogues.

Tony. So clap hands. [*All embrace.*]

Toby. What say you, merchant, as a merry jest and in proof of your good-will, shall we beg one voluntary gift from you?

Tony. Reflect, sir, we have given you your life; a small exchange —

Toby. Tut, tut, brother, you are too serious; I meant some trifling remembrance of so generous a gentleman and so skilled a fighter.

Merchant. As you will; I could refuse you little.

Tony. Then must we make it so very little that you could not.

Toby [*aside to* Tony]. My dear brother, you do not know him. He could refuse a penny to a beggar.

The Loyal Two

[*Aloud.*] What say you to the first living thing that meets you on your return? Dog, cat — we will treat it kindly for your sake.

Merchant. A happy thought. The first live thing of mine that greets me, I will send straightway.

Tony. O noble merchant! Now for the road home; we will see you on your way.   [*Exeunt, R.*

Enter ROGER *and* MILES, *L.*

Roger. Here, where the ways divide, we part. It is settled, then, that during our adventures we withhold our names, that we follow up whatever offers, and a year and a day hence, at latest, meet on this spot to recount all happenings.

Miles. And that if either be in danger the other come to his aid.

Roger. How shall we know of danger?

Miles. That we must leave to Fate, who ever befriends those that trust her veiled face. And we are not for nothing twins.

Roger. Farewell, brother. Oh, my heart fails me! If you were in danger —

Miles. You would know it. Why, Roger, this will never do!

Roger. You are right, Miles. The day passes; I must go. [*Exit, R.*

Enter, L., MARIAN, *singing.*

Marian.

    The lark is up in the merry morn,
      The cuckoo cries at noon,
    But the nightingale on the budding thorn
      Sings only to the moon.

Miles. Here is my adventure. O loveliest lady —

Marian. My gentle sir, whoever you be, this is no place for you. Do not stop to talk, the woods have more robbers in them than wild beasts; make haste out, for if night catches you here, you will have worse than night to deal with. You are likely to lose purse and life together. Do not speak, but go.

Miles. Your word is my law, though it were death.

Marian. Do not betray me, as I for you have betrayed my companions. Hush, obey!

Miles. Give me, if I must go, some proof that this has not been a dream.

Marian. Here is my chain; wear it if you will, but oh, go, go! · [*Exit* MILES, *R.*

    [*Sings.*]

    The woodthrush sings in the shadow cool
      The livelong summer morn;

30

" Here is my chain ; wear it if you will, but oh, go, go ! "

The Loyal Two

But the nightingale is in love, poor fool,
   With her breast against the thorn.

Heigh-ho the nightingale !   I'll go look for a thorn.
   [*Sings.*]
      But the nightingale is in love, poor fool,
         With her breast against the thorn.

[Exit, L.

CURTAIN

ACT II

SCENE: *Before the* MERCHANT'S *House.*

Enter CLOWN.

Clown. There has been no sleep in the house this night. Here has been my young mistress in tears, her waiting-woman in hysterics, the house in an uproar, pepper in the soup, the cook in a rage, and a cold in my head. If my old master had lost his head instead of his way, or caught the plague instead of a possible rheumatism, there could not be more to-do. Although he has been six years away, they cannot wait six hours now to see him. What is that cloud of dust? My master, I'll be bound. I'll in and call my mistress. [*Exit, R.*

The Loyal Two

Enter MERCHANT, *L.*

Merchant. At last, after many dangers, I see my own house again. Years of absence have changed me, but not it.

Enter MIRA, *R.*

Mira. Father! [*They embrace.*]

Merchant. My only, my beloved child! [*Suddenly.*] Oh, what have I done? O despair!

Mira. Dear father, what is it? What distresses you?

Merchant. Do I see you but to lose you? and how terribly!

Mira. You frighten me. Come in and rest; then tell me your grief. [*Exeunt, R.*

Enter FAN *and* CLOWN, *R.*

Fan. Deny it no more. I saw you in the pantry.

Clown. Was there not pepper in the soup? I deny the whole. How did you see me?

Fan. With these eyes of mine.

Clown. They are wills-o'-the-wisp.

Fan. I do not know any Will, but I know I saw you.

Clown. You know one will — one will you love.

Fan. What do you mean?

Clown. Your own. We all have cause to know it.

Fan. Whom do you mean by Will-o'-the-wisp?

Clown. I'll prove it if you will hold your peace about the pantry; it would put master in a blind rage — but, oh, he'd find my back all right!

Fan. Then prove it well.

Clown. Will-o'-the-wisp misleads all passers-by. You passed by, your eyes misled you for I was not there; I say, therefore, your eyes are wills-o'-the-wisp. [*Exeunt, R.*

Enter MIRA *and* MERCHANT, *R.*

Mira. Dear father, your honor is pledged, which is far dearer to me than my own happiness. I will set out at once to redeem your word, taking only the clown for company. No one will molest a lonely and unhappy girl.

Merchant. O fatal wood which has cost me both my children! Mira, you shall not go. I will return instead myself.

Mira. Your promise, father. Be firm; I am. [*Weeping.*] O dear house where I have so happily awaited my father's coming! Farewell, dear father; think of me.   [*Exit, L.*

Enter CLOWN, *R.*

Merchant. Do you hear, fool? Follow your mistress and guard her with your life.

Clown. I would rather guard her with a stout stick. My poor pretty mistress!   [*Exit L. Exit* MERCHANT, *R.*

Enter ROGER, *L.*

Roger. No adventure yet. I wonder if Miles has found one; the wood is likelier than the city. Heigh-ho, I am tired and hungry. Here is a friendly door. [*Knocks.*]

Enter MERCHANT, *R.*

Merchant. Sir, your servant.

Roger. Your servant, sir. Can you direct me to a bed and a breakfast, or rather, since it's some twelve hours too late for that question, to a seat and a dinner?

Merchant. My house is at your service. Fan!

Enter FAN, *R.*

Show this gentleman to the blue room and tell the cook that we have a guest to dinner. Only one guest, mind.

Fan. Is this a day for a party, master, when my sweet young mistress —? [*Weeps.*] The bread will be salt with all our tears.

Merchant [*in a rage*]. Then shall we eat the less.

Roger. You are in grief, sir. I would not tax you with my presence at such a time.

Merchant. For the grief there will be long time, but for hospitality the present moment is never too early. I pray you go in.

[*Exeunt* ROGER *and* FAN, *R.*
My heart is heavy, and he looks as if he had a fearful appetite. O my poor Mira!

[*Weeps, his face hidden in his right arm; his whole body is shaken.*

Enter ROGER, *R.*

Roger. I have the story now, and I will restore your daughter to you or perish in saving her.

Merchant. Do you understand the danger? The two are part of a large band.

The Loyal Two

Roger. Danger is but the wing whereon the adventurous lifts himself to achievement. Farewell, and hope.   [*Exit* ROGER, *L.*

Merchant. Oh, farewell! Success be yours. I will go pray.   [*Exit* MERCHANT, *R.*

CURTAIN

ACT III

SCENE: *Same as Act I.*

Enter TONY *and* TOBY, *L.*

Tony. What is to be done? She will neither eat nor smile.

Toby. From a dog that won't bark, a man that won't drink, and a woman that won't laugh, may Heaven preserve me!

Tony. There's white magic in the girl; she has tamed my heart.

Toby. Humph, she could easier tame a sharp and treacherous little fox. Yonder she comes. I'll fetch my lute and try some conjuring. [*Exit, R.*

The Loyal Two

Enter MIRA, *L.*

Mira.   Are there no other people in this wood?

Tony.   Yes, mistress, a great band of robbers, than whom a pack of wolves is civiler, and for whom we have small respect. They are, as you might say, common or garden thieves, who steal only by the light of nature, which is to say by moonlight.

Mira.   Wherein do you differ?

Tony.   We live by our wits, and rob with our brains rather than our fists.

Enter TOBY, *R.*

Toby.   Will you hear a song, mistress?

Mira.   I must if you choose to sing.

Toby   [*sings*].

> Oh, a merry thing is a greenwood life!
> With nimble wits and ready knife
> We cut a purse or steal a wife,
>   And we never miss nor dally.
> We always spend and we never save,
> For meat and drink are all we crave,
> A suit of green, — and, last, a grave
>   In a green and hidden valley.

Mira.   I thank you for your kind intent.

Tony.   Now, a dance !   [*The two dance wildly.*]

Enter ROGER, *R.*

Roger. Halt there! Are not you the rascals that have robbed a father of his daughter?

Toby. That we be, master, and he was as great a niggard of her beauty as of his gold.

Tony. Very honest rascals both, and, I make no doubt, better men than you.

Roger. Shall we try that?

Tony. With all my heart.

Toby. A perfect brotherhood — one heart between two.

Roger. But not one arm. Which of you comes first?

Toby. The gentleman is wise; two to one spoils sport.

Tony. I must come first, for you would not leave enough for me to finish.

Toby. So be it. Now, Fortune favor her minions.

Tony. She must, lest we forswear her and turn honest men. Are you ready, sir? [*They fight;* TONY *is wounded.*] Enough, enough. My legs, like ungrateful sons, refuse to support me.

Roger. Then to the almshouse with you. Come on, you, if you dare.

The Loyal Two

Toby. I am for you. [*They fight*; TOBY *is wounded.*] Fortune's a fickle girl and to-day she sulks. But though she is my only love, perhaps she is jealous of the other sullen beauty. To-morrow we are only Fortune's. But that there may be a to-morrow, you must help us to our legs, since our legs will not help us but traitorously bend before the conqueror. [*They stagger off, L.*]

Roger. Sullen, hah? Then I'll none of her, send her safely home and seek further; a lowering adventure is none for me. [*Turns.*] Sullen, what? She is more dazzling than an April dawn!

Mira. Sir, my servitude is changed. I pray you prove no worse master than those limping rogues.

Roger. Changed into freedom, dear lady. I am your eternal servitor — oh, might I be not less than your husband!

Mira. That is as my father shall say.

Roger. He can refuse me nothing that you shall ask.

Mira. Then there is my hand. I can hardly pause to talk, I so long to see him.

Roger. Had you not a servant?

Mira. He, poor fellow, disappeared. And he is very faithful.

Roger. You shall have him again. Here, Tony, Toby, see this lady on her way.

[*Enter* TONY *and* TOBY, *L., limp across the stage, and exeunt R., followed by* MIRA.]

Enter MARIAN, *L.*

Marian [*sings*].

> From hour to hour the saucy jay
>   Mocks at himself in the pool;
> But the nightingale on the blossomy spray
>   Is in love — in love — poor fool!

My gentleman again! Oh, why are you so mad?

Roger. Fair lady —

Marian. Did not I persuade you to leave the wood, if not for your own sake, then for mine? Your eyes promised obedience; are not such silent pledges sacred?

Roger. A stronger motive, madam, called me hither.

Marian. What could be stronger than my direct command? You look strangely at me — where is my chain? Oh, can a man forget so soon? [*Exit, L.*

Roger. My brother's adventure seems well under way.

The Loyal Two

Enter ROBBERS, *L.*

1st Robber.   You are our prisoner.

Roger.   You must prove that.

1st Robber.   On your back.

Roger.   You will not see my back.

[*They fight until* ROBBERS *lie in heaps, entering
one at a time, L., and falling in the centre of
the stage.   At last* ROGER *falls.*]

Villains, I am not yet dead!

CURTAIN

45

ACT IV

Scene: *Same as Act II.*

Enter Merchant *and* Fan, *R.*

Merchant. No news as yet. In that terrible wood what can one man do? I should have held him back, his blood is on me. Hark! Who called?

Fan. It was only a crow flying overhead.

Merchant. Each hour is a century long, and yet my death comes never the sooner. Surely I heard a voice.

Fan. It was a dog in the next street, master.

Merchant. What figure is that in the distance? O old dim eyes! It is — it is my child!

[*Rushes off, L.*

46

The Loyal Two

Fan. · They see better than mine, but mine are blinded with joy. It is my young mistress indeed. [*Weeps.*]

Enter MERCHANT *and* MIRA, *L.*

Mira [*embraces* FAN. *To* MERCHANT]. But you have not yet asked how came this unhoped return.

Merchant. It is enough that you are returned.

Fan. Humph, the deliverer may not think so.

Mira. It was a young adventurer.

Fan. I'll be sworn it was our man.

Merchant. I know, I know. We spoke of you.

Mira. He overcame my captors one by one and restored me to happiness — and to love.

Merchant. Eh? eh? To your father, you mean.

Mira. Dear father, I knew you would feel no reward too great for him.

Merchant [*in a panic*]. How? how? how?

Mira. So I promised him even my hand.

Merchant. Quite right. But of course you did not hint at a dowry.

Mira. He never thought of such a thing, nor did I.

Fan. Don't be too sure; he's a clever one.

Merchant. Where is the young man? Why is he not come to receive his reward?

Mira. The poor faithful clown was lost, and the adventurer went to seek him.

Fan. Alackaday! That was throwing the hatchet after the helve.

Merchant. Dear me, I hope nothing will happen; it is not every day one gets a son-in-law who does not want a dowry. What's his name?

Mira. I — I did not ask him.

Merchant. Be sure you ask him now, for yonder he comes.

Enter MILES, *L., the chain on.*

Mira [*running to him*]. Safe, and thrice, thrice welcome, my love. But where is the clown?

Miles. Clown? I saw no clown.

Mira. O my poor, faithful fellow! He is dead then.

Miles. Dead? Nonsense! He will be here all right.

Merchant. Daughter, let me speak. Sir, we owe you gratitude which we can never hope to pay.

Fan. Catch him trying! [*Exit, R.*

Merchant. And yet my daughter's hand is perhaps no mean recompense for even your achievements.

Miles. I — ah — of course. Immensely honoured, sir. Your goodness overpowers me. [*Walks aside.*]
I am taken for Roger; but where is Roger?

The Loyal Two

Merchant. Daughter, you and this gentleman will have much to say to each other. I leave you.

[*Exit, R.*

Mira. At last we are alone. O my deliverer, when last we met, fear tied my tongue, but my eyes did double duty. I could not have mistaken you had we been twenty years apart.

Miles. You have a good eye, madam.

Mira. Ah, you would have remembered as long, would you not, the hand I laid in yours, yielding you gratitude and something more?

Miles. So fair a hand could never be forgotten.

Mira. Is it not? For it holds much gold. Do not tell me my father's great wealth makes you timid. He loves me well, for I am now, alas! his only child.

Miles. I am not naturally timid, madam, but the suddenness of our meeting — I had not known this was your house.

Mira. But now it is yours, and all that is in it.

Miles. Dear lady, you are too good to a wanderer. But your clown calls me away. I must show my gratitude by service. I will not stop to eat or drink.

Mira. I fear he is dead.

Miles. No, no. He cannot be. No farewell, or

I shall not have the resolution to go. Leave me, dear lady, or I shall never leave this spot.

Mira. Farewell. [*Exit, R.*

Miles. Whew! And I don't even know her name. Now to find Roger — in that maze of a wood, I make no doubt.

Enter MARIAN, *L.*

My wood-girl!

Marian. Sir!

Miles. Do you not know me?

Marian. A thought too well.

Miles. Oh, not half well enough. I have virtues, when you look for them.

Marian. You have other qualities that do not stay for searching. I am not keen to rummage farther.

Miles. Dear lady —

Marian. My name is Marian.

Miles. Dear Marian —

Marian. Sir!

Miles. O woman, girl, what you will, what does this mean? I have done nothing.

Marian. What you do is nothing to me.

Miles. Those two nothings should make something. I do not know what I have done, but I am sorry. Forgive me!

50

The Loyal Two

Marian. I think — not. [*Aside.*] There is my chain. Well! [*Aloud.*] Maybe, if you ask often enough. But how did you escape from the robbers?

Miles. Oh, I see! Robbers, eh? Why, I can't stay here, dear Marian. I will tell you when I see you again. [*Exit, L.*

CURTAIN

ACT V

SCENE: *Same as the last.*

Enter MARIAN, *R.*

Marian. After questioning at every door, I find that this is the rich merchant's house whose daughter was stolen long ago by robbers. What! it is the house where I saw my young adventurer. My heart tolls for trouble; well, let that pass. Now, if the clown's story be true, I shall find in this next moment a father at once and a sister. [*Knocks.*]

Enter FAN, *R.*

Fan. Mistress!

Marian. I would speak with your master.

Fan. Enter.   [*Exeunt, R.*

The Loyal Two

Enter ROGER *and* CLOWN, *L.*

Roger. Now, fellow, hold your tongue about what you have seen.

Clown. Truth, sir, I am not sure what I did see and whether I only saw double.

Roger. That is well. Where is Miles?

Clown. He fell back to look in the town for some one, he said.

Roger. As for your strange story about the daughter lost so long, reared up among the robbers, and at your mere word setting out to find her father, — the event shall prove the truth of all.

Clown. Oh, sir, in looking at her I seemed to see double again, and the image of her mother before me as she lived.

Enter MIRA, *R.*

Mira. What voice did I hear? Oh, sir, are you come again?

Roger. So cold a greeting, Mira? Can you not say, "Dear Roger, I am glad of your safety"?

Mira. That am I — but — but, you were cold yourself when we last said good-by.

Roger. "Last said?" Ah, Mira, are you so sure? Who comes from the house?

Enter MARIAN, *R.*

Mira. My recovered sister. This is a day of almost too great happiness.

Marian. My friend, have you nothing to say?

Roger. A loving greeting, dear sister.

Marian. Sister? Mira! Oh, sister, trust him not; he is altogether false.

Mira. Here is some terrible mistake. Dear Marian, he is my promised husband.

Marian. Let him give me back my chain which he wears — he wore. My chain! Take it out, sir, from wherever it is hidden, and restore it. Oh, my chain!

Mira. Roger, can this be so?

Roger. Oh, hush, sweet! I must not explain till my time comes; only trust me a moment longer.

Clown. Old mistress and new mistress, have you no words for your long-lost fool? You have not wanted folly, I see.

Mira. Ah, friend, you jest with a tear in your eye.

Clown. I'd rather it was there than on my lip, for I never loved salt water.

Enter MILES, *L.*

Mira. Roger! I did not see you go. Two Rogers!

Marian. I see it all now. Brother, forgive my

54

" Ladies, my blessing is for you."

The Loyal Two

anger; and from you [*to* MILES] I must have greater forgiveness — of my mistrust.

Miles. Dear Marian ! I may call you, now, so ?

Enter MERCHANT, *R.*

Sir, you have found a daughter only to lose her, for she is mine. You will not grudge her me so long as I ask nothing along with her.

Merchant. I bless you both, my gallant sons.

Clown.

> Ladies, my blessing is for you,
> And for that dower which is your due
> I give the richest of my store ;
> Of wisdom much, of folly more.
> Of wisdom, all that you can share ;
> Of folly, all you cannot spare ; —
> Wisdom is beauteous in a wife,
> And folly is the salt of life.

CURTAIN

COLUMBINE'S MARRIAGE

PUPPETS

MERCHANT, *Columbine's father.* Dark dress, purse at girdle.

DR. WISEMAN ⎫
CAPTAIN BRAZENNOSE ⎬ *her suitors.*
LEANDER ⎭

Black suit, bands, shovel hat, sword.
Dress of a soldier, sword.
Court dress.

HARLEQUIN ⎫
⎬ *strolling players.*
PIERROT ⎭

Tight-fitting suit of red and green lozenges ; flute or flageolet.
Clown's dress.

COLUMBINE. Court dress of red and gold.

FLOWER-DE-LUCE, *a gypsy girl.* Gypsy dress, blue or lavender, with yellow or brown ; knife.

Properties : flute, knife, coin.

Columbine's Marriage

ACT I

Scene: *A Public Place.*

Enter Harlequin *and* Pierrot, *L.*

Pierrot [*sings.*]
> My father was a piper's son,
> He used to play when day was done,
> But all the tune that he could play
> Was, " Over the hills and far away."

Harlequin.
> Over the hills where the sunset lies,
> Till the stars grow pale and the night wind dies.
>
> The birds that wing their way through the blue
> Direct my feet to the strange and new;
> And the open road lies straight and free,
> It calls and calls till it tortures me.

61

Both.

> Over the hills and far away
> We follow the dying, dawning day.

Harlequin. Enough, Pierrot. A door is opening yonder, and out come two gentlemen of the sort that would rather hear the parrot than the nightingale, because the former states a fact.

Pierrot. Pierrot wants his dinner.

Harlequin. I'll back your nose to lead you to the best kitchen as I'd trust a hound to find the fox. When you have fixed on an inn, come back for me.

[*Exit* PIERROT, *R.* HARLEQUIN *retires, L.*

Enter MERCHANT *and* DR. WISEMAN, *R.*

Merchant. If there went but one word to a bargain, Doctor, you would have been a bridegroom this month since.

Dr. Wiseman. My excellent friend, which is to say surpassing, it is not my word which has been wanting to this affair. *Paucis verbis*, though an excellent saying, is not here applicable.

Merchant. There you say simple truth, for you have talked me deaf, dumb, and blind.

Dr. Wiseman. Then what hinders, I pray, or

Columbine's Marriage

delays, or it may be prevents, that my overlong courtship should end in a speedy marriage? I am not
of the antediluvian race that I should woo a hundred
years or so, nor is your daughter another Penelope to
keep her suitors hanging for twenty years by a thread.

Merchant. To do justice to Columbine, she fancies,
I think, her mother's favourite as little as mine. It's
her mother, Doctor, her mother, that is all for marrying her girl to the Captain.

Dr. Wiseman. Captain Brazennose is a braggart
and a bully, a boaster, sir, a braggadocio.

Merchant. Softly, Doctor, softly. He has served
with distinction in the wars.

Dr. Wiseman. This is his story, sir, or his tale or
account of himself. Saw you ever any one that knew
him notoriously in the camp or the field? And you,
sir, if you were as the vulgar say, master in your own
house, he would not at this instant be, sir, drinking
your wine, beating your servants, and courting your
daughter.

Merchant. I am a patient man, and, as you well
know, your steady friend; but my patience has its limits.

Dr. Wiseman. I would that my courtship had. I
would fain write *finis* to this first volume and start on
the second, which is called matrimony.

Enter Captain Brazennose, *L.*

Captain Brazennose. What, merchant, not gone yet? I warrant when your fortune was a-making you did not stand to gossip thus.

Merchant. My affair is now with my esteemed friend, Dr. Wiseman.

Captain Brazennose. Hah! hah! I should not have taken the good gentleman for a man of affairs.

Dr. Wiseman. In my capacity, sir, as a man of learning, of erudition, sir, or of science, which is to say wisdom, I find all affairs to be my province.

Captain Brazennose. Indeed, Doctor, do not you find some of them insubordinate provinces?

Merchant [*anxiously*]. Come, come! Doctor, will you walk with me?

Dr. Wiseman. A little way; but if this military gentleman, or warlike, or belligerent, sir, will await me, we will hold some slight discourse touching the province of wisdom, to which the marches and the entering in, sir [*to* Captain Brazennose], is that a man should guard his tongue or keep or hold— [*Voice dies away as he follows* Merchant *off, R.*]

Harlequin [*coming forward*]. Captain, your friend seems a man not of words only, but of spirit, perhaps even of deeds.

Columbine's Marriage

Captain Brazennose. I make no account of that. I have dealt with twenty such before breakfast.

Harlequin. I see you are not afraid of his long words.

Captain Brazennose. My sword will reach farther. Tut, tut, they are but breath, like the wind that whistles in a man's ears. I will walk a little way to limber my legs. [*Exit, L.*

Enter LEANDER *and* COLUMBINE, *R.* HARLEQUIN *retires, L.*

Leander. Dearest Columbine, I thought you would never come.

Columbine. I thought so, too, Leander, but changed my thought.

Leander. Cruel girl, why will you not be kind? You cannot prefer to my unselfish devotion the mercenary soldier's or the equally mercenary pedant's pretensions?

Columbine. They are, I admit, equally detestable; but why should I prefer Leander? How can I know him less interested, or only less frankly so?

Leander. My own heart acquits me, but against your unjust suspicion I can offer but my bare word.

Columbine. Your word, dear Leander, is enough.

[*He moves to embrace her.*]   Softly, softly, sir. I don't think I want to marry.

Leander.   Columbine, I am, it is true, poor, but not a beggar while I have the house of my ancestors and an unstained sword. I would not have you driven into my arms by persecution, my own or another's, and you shall not hear the unwelcome word again from me. Some one is coming — go in, my love.

Columbine.   I thought you just said, Leander, I was not to hear the word.

Leander.   Not that word. Oh, I don't promise to stop loving, only asking.   [*Exit* COLUMBINE, *R.*

Enter PIERROT, *R.*

Pierrot [*running into* LEANDER].   Your servant, sir.

Leander.   None of mine. Folly is not my livery.

Pierrot.   No, sir, you wear it within; I, mine all on the outside. Your servant, sir.

Leander [*giving money*].   Here's for your wit.

[*Exit, R.*

Harlequin.   Let me see. Gold? The poor lad has none to spare; we must do him for this a good turn. His mistress is pestered by a pair of foolish suitors that I have a mind to relieve him of.

[*Exit with* PIERROT, *L.*

Columbine's Marriage

Enter DR. WISEMAN.

Dr. Wiseman. O Columbine, into what dangers and perils does your fortune draw us poor mortals! I have an incalculable aversion to the sight of steel; yet I carry here a sword as big as a weaver's beam to serve me withal defensively and offensively, to wit, against the heavy hand of a full-bellied cutthroat and the silly heart of an empty-headed female.

Enter HARLEQUIN, *L.*

Harlequin [*speaking into the wings*]. Go meet him, Pierrot. Good day, grave sir. If you are of the acquaintance of Dr. Wiseman, I pray you tell me where he may be found.

Dr. Wiseman. You have him, sir, in your organ of recognition, which the vulgar call your sight.

Harlequin. Then I warn you, sir, to beware of that instrument of execution, which the vulgar call a sword.

Dr. Wiseman. I see no sword.

Harlequin. Here is your own, and if you could see around three corners, your excellency would perceive that of Captain Brazennose, who invites you by my lips to mortal combat.

Comedies and Legends for Marionettes

Dr. Wiseman. My profession, sir, is peace, which I not only profess but practise, and my learning is of too inestimable a value for the world to be sacrificed in an idle quarrel, a falling out, or dispute.

Harlequin. Your learning will be little esteemed in the world if it be known you cannot defend it.

Dr. Wiseman. I will defend it against all comers, in Greek, in Latin, in Aramaic, or Syrian, or Ethiopian, or in any of the tongues of Pentecost.

Harlequin. You need not so many syllables, Doctor, one will suffice; you are a man of letters, Doctor, but five letters will fill your wants — s-t-e-e-l.

Dr. Wiseman. I will defend it, I say, but by the tongue, sir; by the lips, teeth, larynx, and epiglottis, which signifies, in brief, with words.

Harlequin. In this case, Doctor, you must defend it in Samson's manner with the bone of the jaw, or else at length, which is to say, with a sword; for the Captain has taken your former words in very ill part.

Dr. Wiseman. I am a merciful man. I would not cut him off in the midst of his evil living.

Harlequin. Walk this way, sir; I will show you reasons.   [*Exeunt, R.*

68

Columbine's Marriage

Enter PIERROT *and* CAPTAIN BRAZENNOSE, *L.*

Captain Brazennose. Now, by blood and bones, I think there is no sense in fighting with a miserable pedant, nor no fun neither.

Pierrot. He thinks not so. You spoke shortly to him but now, and he demands satisfaction.

Captain Brazennose. Counsel him more wisely, my good fellow. I should spit him as boys do butterflies.

Pierrot. Then he will be impaled on the point of honour. He is very resolute. Oh, Captain, these men of ink and words are marvellous bloody-minded!

Captain Brazennose. Zounds! He's not more bloody-minded than I. Bid him come. But hold [*catching* PIERROT *as he starts*]. I recall that the fair Columbine has looked on him with a gentle air, as it were disdainful-kind, and what she has smiled on for me is sacred.

Pierrot. There, Captain, your heart may be at ease. She detests him as much as you, and endures him only out of obedience.

Captain Brazennose. Carry him my acceptance of instant and mortal duello. Yet stay, the danger is too great of interruption here; we must wait for a more convenient time and place.

Pierrot. Have no care. I will keep watch that no one passes.

Enter Dr. Wiseman *and* Harlequin, *R.*

Harlequin. How is your patient, Pierrot?

Pierrot. Very impatient, sir. I can scarce hold him from immediate flight. And yours?

Harlequin. Nearly dead of fear. Come, Doctor, my friend says the Captain will not be appeased. Now show him that the sword in your hand is mightier than the pen.

Pierrot. Captain, I have assured him that you meant no offence, but he says you gentlemen of the sword think nobody but themselves can have a ticklish honour.

Dr. Wiseman [*as* Harlequin *pushes him to the centre of the stage*]. Captain Brazennose, I feel it my duty, my obligation or behoof, sir, to warn you that, though not easily moved and stirred, I am a dangerous enemy.

Captain Brazennose. [*Similar business with* Pierrot.] Blood and wounds, Dr. Wiseman, do you think to trifle with an approved soldier like myself?

Dr. Wiseman. I am a merciful man, Captain, and the merciful man is merciful to his beast. If honour

" I am a dangerous enemy."

could be appeased in any honourable way, fashion, or manner —

Pierrot. Do you hear? He calls you a beast, Captain Brazennose. [*To* DOCTOR.] I hope your will is made and your library devised where it will do good, for you will read in it no more —

Harlequin. No more words.

Dr. Wiseman [*to* HARLEQUIN]. What — what does that mean?

Harlequin. That it is the moment for deeds. Pierrot, place your man.

Pierrot [*pacing off the ground*]. There you are, Captain. Your experience in the eighty-three duels you told me of —

Harlequin. Are you ready, gentlemen?

Captain Brazennose. Thunder and battle, we delay too long!

Harlequin. When I say three, begin. One — two —

Dr. Wiseman. I must sharpen my sword first.

[*Exit, R.*

Captain Brazennose. I feel somewhat unwell. I will take a turn and be back.

Harlequin. There's a good deed consummated. Follow your man, Pierrot, and see that his cour-

age does not boil up again. [*Exit* PIERROT, *L.*]
Heigh-ho! The pretty child will be left in peace.
[*Sings.*]

> A rare bright flower beneath the trees,
>> Hey, nonny, nonny!
> Dipped and danced to the wayward breeze,
> Scarlet and gold and full of honey,
> Glad to the eye and sweet for the bees,
>> Hey, nonny, nonny!
>
> A wanderer caught in a soft spring shower,
>> Hey, nonny, nonny!
> Stayed at the tree and stooped to the flower;
> He plucked for his bosom the blossom bonny,
> But the flower was dead within the hour,
>> Hey, nonny, nonny!

Enter COLUMBINE, *R.*

Columbine. Who sings?

Harlequin. A wayfarer, lady — one of those strange
creatures who show all faces and own none: the
mirror of folly, the thief of laughter, the ape of
nature, who supply to children wonder, to men mock-
ery, and to old age recollection. I am, madam, a
strolling player.

Columbine. You have a sweet voice.

Columbine's Marriage

Harlequin. You might truly call it a golden voice, for it feeds and clothes me.

Columbine. What, then, is left for your wit to do?

Harlequin. Get me out of the scrapes my voice gets me into.

Columbine. Nay, if you rhyme I cannot follow you.

Harlequin. Would you follow me without rhyme or reason?

Columbine [*aside*]. I could follow you without wisdom and duty. Oh, Leander, you should not have left me! [*To him.*] Are you kin, sir, to the Pied Piper of Hamelin, that you hold yourself so certain of a following?

Harlequin. When I pipe, lady, it is not the rats that run after.

Columbine. Your coat is pied.

Harlequin. And so was his.

Columbine. His heart was not; it was black as the century-living crow.

Harlequin. And mine is pied like the meadows when cloud shadows race over. [*Sings.*]

My father was the piper's son,
He played o' his pipe till day was done,
His heart was wild as the winds that say:
"Come over the hills and far away!"

Over the hilltops, over and on,
Till the dawn-wind wakes and the stars are gone.

Columbine. How dark it grows! Something is tugging at my heart strings.

Harlequin. Go in, child, night is coming on. The hollows in the hills are full of darkness which rises slowly, slowly like a tide till the whole world is drowned in dreams. Go in to your mother and the fire.

Enter PIERROT, *R.*

Columbine [*starting*]. Ah! [*Exit, R.*
Pierrot. Comrade, we must up and out. Whom d'ye think I saw in the village?

Harlequin. Who's that? Oh, Pierrot, I did not know your white coat in the dusk!

Pierrot. Eh, dreaming again! Whom think you I saw?

Harlequin. A rat! [*Bursting into laughter.*] How the foul fiend do I know?

Pierrot. Worse than the fiend — Flower-de-Luce.

Harlequin. The gypsy girl —

Pierrot. That swore she'd marry you —

Harlequin. Whether or no! Right, Pierrot, we'll on, for she might do it.

76

Columbine's Marriage

Both [*sing*].

> Over the hills and far away,
> Follow, follow the dying day.

[Exeunt, L.

CURTAIN

ACT II

S<small>CENE</small> : *A Great Deserted Hall, Doors all around it.*

Enter H<small>ARLEQUIN</small> *and* P<small>IERROT</small>, *R.*

Pierrot. Eh, comrade, how's this for luck? It's cool to-night on the hills.

Harlequin. The moon and the mist are on the hills. Give me my pipe. [*Plays a few bars.*] Strange that there is no one in all this vast old house.

Pierrot. I know the place; its master sticks to his town house like a flea to a dog, preferring rats to robbers, and having a wholesome and pious fear of his progenitors.

Harlequin. This hall is immense as a king's presence chamber, and lonely and splendid as a queen's tomb.

Columbine's Marriage

Pierrot. It has as many doors as King Arthur's Round Table had seats.

Harlequin. Why, that's a score and ten, fellow.

Pierrot. Saving your presence, comrade, it is a round dozen. Sir Launcelot, Sir Gawain, Sir Tristram —

Harlequin. Hark! here come they to answer to the roll.

Pierrot. There are steps this way, surely.

Harlequin. This way, too. Suppose we show the better part of valor.   [*Exeunt, L.*

Enter DR. WISEMAN, *L.,* CAPTAIN BRAZENNOSE, *R., encountering.*

Dr. Wiseman. Merciful powers!

Captain Brazennose. Blood and thunder!

Dr. Wiseman. You, Captain?

Captain Brazennose. You, Doctor?

Dr. Wiseman. Why, yes, Captain, I was looking for you, as who should say, searching.

Captain Brazennose. Ah — hum — oh — to be sure. Doctor, they told me you had come this way. I wanted to resume our arrested combat.

Dr. Wiseman. I lost in the mist, or the fog, first my way and then my sword.

Captain Brazennose. Then, I suppose, as a man of honour, I can't well press you?

Dr. Wiseman. If it had been otherwise or in another circumstance, I should have been most keen. Since we are met now so fortunately, which signifies, Captain, so strangely, I may tell you in confidence that I have put from me the idea of marriage. *Mulier*, sir, which signifies in Latin woman, has to my ears too mulish a sound.

Captain Brazennose. Zounds! that is strange — I had about made up my mind that marriage and a quiet fireside would not suit a soldier.

Dr. Wiseman. Extra-ordinary, Captain Brazennose; I compliment your wisdom.

Captain Brazennose. Hang me, if you are not a cleverer fellow than I took you for! [*Starting up.*] What's that — a ghost?

Dr. Wiseman. If by ghost you mean spirit, Captain, which the word properly signifies, there are two already in the room.

Captain Brazennose. Where? where?

Dr. Wiseman. Yours, most magnanimous military, and mine.

Captain Brazennose. Hah! hah! good joke! But, sir, I'm not afraid of man, ghost, or devil.

Columbine's Marriage

Dr. Wiseman. There be certainly footfalls. Anathema — spirits, I defy ye! Captain, suppose we search for some place smaller and more commodious, or as the vulgar say, snug quarters.

Captain Brazennose. Aye, Doctor, I have faced many ghosts — but, as you say, snug quarters!

[*Exeunt, R.*

Enter HARLEQUIN *and* PIERROT, *L.*

Harlequin. The knights were worth seeing.

Pierrot. If I were you, comrade, I'd not speak so loud.

Harlequin. · Why, you're not afraid of ghosts?

Pierrot. I am uncommonly afraid of Flower-de-Luce.

Harlequin. Hold your tongue, fool, or, as before, you'll raise her — oh, thunder!

Enter FLOWER-DE-LUCE, *R.*

Pierrot. Oh, lightning! I'm off. [*Exit, L.*

Flower-de-Luce. Well, what have you to say?

Harlequin. Nothing, my dear. An Eastern mute is more conversible than I to-night.

Flower-de-Luce. Are you not surprised to see me?

Harlequin. No more than summer when she hears the cuckoo, or he that hath smelled the sweet breath of a panther when the tawny beast leaps on him. I can always expect you — and death.

Flower-de-Luce. You would rather have seen the other.

Harlequin. My dear, you sometimes make me think that.

Flower-de-Luce. We have said all of this a score of times.

Harlequin. Life, Flower-de-Luce, is a play; we are all players and must enact our parts or well or ill; but with these manifold rehearsals you and I should in time reach perfection.

Flower-de-Luce. Look at me, Harlequin; am I not beautiful?

Harlequin [*enthusiastically*]. You are radiant.

Flower-de-Luce. Then why not marry me?

Harlequin. Marry, sweetheart, because I do not love. Now, my splendid-scornful inquisitress, it is my turn at the question. Have I ever said I did?

Flower-de-Luce. No, and a curse upon the no.

Harlequin. Reflect, lass; true it is marriage is a sacrament, the fireside is warm, home is a good place, children are better than lands and gold, a wife is a part of a man's own heart. But then marriage is a yoke, and the fireside is very narrow. For home you

may have the wide world; for children the keen white stars; for spouse the wind that bloweth where it listeth. Yet if you will to wedlock, wed whom you will so it be not Harlequin, for no man can escape his destiny. Take Captain Brazennose. Take Dr. Wiseman. Take even Pierrot. But for me —
[*Sings.*]
> The long white road runs straight and free,
> It calls and calls till it tortures me.

Flower-de-Luce. I hear the call; it is in the gypsy blood, and I have to wander.

Harlequin. Why not wander, then?

Flower-de-Luce. Eh, Harlequin, you piped while I danced, and now whether I will or no I have to follow. When I tire of following, do you know what I shall do?

Harlequin. Stop, I hope.

Flower-de-Luce. I'll stop your piping with my little knife here.

Harlequin. My lovely girl, if that is all, pray use your little knife now.

Flower-de-Luce. No, no — I'm not tired yet. But I'm sleepy — good night. [*Exit, L.*

Harlequin. When the wind gets up, I have to pipe; when the tide catches me, I must sing whether I will or no — till Flower-de-Luce puts in her little knife. Till then, forward! [*Sings.*]

> Over the hills and a great way on,
> The wind blows out of the gates of the sun.

Enter PIERROT, *L.*

Pierrot. Forward's the word, comrade. Where's Flower-de-Luce?

Harlequin. Asleep, I pray. We must be gone before —

Columbine [*outside, sings*].

> Over the hills and far away
> Follow the night that ends in day.

Enter COLUMBINE, *R.*

Harlequin. Powers of mercy!

Columbine. The moon and the mist are on the hills. 'Tis clear as morning, but something colder.

Harlequin. Columbine!

Columbine. I heard your song, and the little cry of your pipe rang in my ears, so I had to follow.

Harlequin. Alone you came?

Columbine. Yes. It is very late.

Harlequin. You are tired, child.

Columbine. So tired, I think I'll go sleep. [*Exit, R.*

84

Columbine's Marriage

Pierrot. Whew! Here's a pretty kettle of fish.

Harlequin. My faith, I thought for a moment she would open Flower-de-Luce's door.

Pierrot. Count on me; but I am marvellous drowsy. *[Exit, L.*

Harlequin. There are, according to some learned Rabbins, seven thousand and nine kinds of evil spirits; but Flower-de-Luce is more dangerous than any. Angry women are worse than two mountain cats.

Enter COLUMBINE, *R.*

Columbine. I cannot sleep. The room is full of moonlight. My heart is too big for my bosom. When you look at me so, I know I have done wrong.

Harlequin. Very wrong, girl, but as soon as it is day we will carry you home again, and when you wake in your own bed you will have forgotten all of this.

Columbine. I shall remember it in dreams.

Harlequin. And in dreams you will hear the same song still. *[Enter* FLOWER-DE-LUCE.*]* *[Aside.]* Now for it! *[To* COLUMBINE.*]* One moment, sweet. *[To* FLOWER-DE-LUCE.*]* My golden lass, why cannot you sleep? Your eyes will be heavy to-morrow.

Flower-de-Luce. Who's that?

Harlequin. A child from the town who lost herself and has been wandering on the hills since sunset in the mist.

Columbine [*to* HARLEQUIN]. Oh, Harlequin, who is that wild, beautiful girl? Her bright eyes make me afraid.

Harlequin. She, too, is a comedian, a companion long since of mine.

Flower-de-Luce. I cannot hang on your words here forever. I must speak with you, Harlequin.

Harlequin [*to her*]. Princess of wild maids and perfect mistress of wayfarers, have not we spoken enough to-night?

Flower-de-Luce. I shall tell her to leave. Child!

Columbine. She looks as though she meant me mischief. [*Aloud.*] I mean no ill.

Harlequin [*to her*]. And shall suffer none.

Flower-de-Luce. This fellow has business with me. We can talk outside. You are not afraid, I suppose, to stay here alone?

Harlequin. Here we can talk well.

Columbine. I will go back to the little room with the moon in it. Which was the door?

Harlequin [*to her*]. Don't stir, dear child, out of my sight, I implore.

Columbine's Marriage

Flower-de-Luce. I'll wait outside for you.

Harlequin [*to her*]. Flower-de-Luce, I must know, before you leave, what you have in your head.

Columbine [*at R. Entrance*]. Good night again, my friend, and you, madam, good night.

Harlequin. Columbine, you'll lose your way again. Stay here, I beg.

Flower-de-Luce [*at L. Entrance*]. I will go take counsel with a trusty friend.

Harlequin [*to her*]. You do not get out without leaving me the little knife.

Flower-de-Luce [*to him*]. You are a fool! We don't part.

Harlequin [*to her*]. All right, my dear, *we* don't part, then.

Flower-de-Luce. Pity there's not another. We might play at cards.

Harlequin. Shall I waken Pierrot, madam?

Columbine. Hark! Did I hear a voice?

Enter PIERROT, *R.*

Pierrot [*to* HARLEQUIN]. The pretty fellow is come seeking Mistress Columbine.

Harlequin. Sooner than I thought. Keep him in talk a moment. [*Exit* PIERROT.] Now, Columbine, here's your door. Go back, and quietly to sleep. When you wake, all will be as it should. Good night, dear child; dream softly. Leander!

[*Exit* COLUMBINE, *R.*

Enter LEANDER, *R.*

Leander. Columbine? Where is she? What have we not suffered! You, sir, shall answer to me.

Harlequin. Come, come, Leander, don't be a fool. I'm your best friend.

Flower-de-Luce. Leander, — since that is your name, — it would be an excellent deed to cut his throat.

Leander. I am marvellously of your opinion, wonderful lady.

Harlequin. For the love of pity, and peace, and charity, and all the other virtues you disdain, Flower-de-Luce, leave us. I have to talk to this man — talk, do you understand, as men talk to men.

Flower-de-Luce. And think they have the entire sum of sense in the world. I wish you, gentlemen, wisdom.

[*Exit, L.*

Leander. I pray you, Harlequin, did you, by chance, save that beautiful girl from drowning?

Harlequin. She could not be more dangerous to

88

Columbine's Marriage

me had I so done.   You would have me divine that I stand in as great danger from you?

Leander.   I am, indeed, your most sworn enemy.

Harlequin.   Then you must shortly be forsworn.

Leander.   My anger is based on just grounds.

Harlequin.   Oh, your anger is groundless, your judgment is baseless, and, like all fiery spirits, yours moves upward to its proper place.

Leander.   Your wit is too quick for me.

Harlequin.   So are my feet too quick for you or any other.   I am, Leander, a wanderer; more restless than the swallow in autumn, more tameless than the unicorn, more swift and subtile than the panther. What!   Ulysses wandered twenty years, but he came home at last.   Æneas travelled even to the gates of Hell, but he built him a kingdom on the other side. I am less stable than Æneas, and like to Ulysses at his life's end, I must up and off again.

Leander.   Indeed, I have heard your song.

Harlequin.   Why, so did Columbine hear it, and it drew her as the fowler draws the bird.   I warned her first.   I watched over her but now.   I waited for you to-night.

Leander.   She shall not be chid —

Harlequin. Nor should be; his destiny no man can change. Take her, she is yours.

Leander. But her parents?

Harlequin. The two suitors have taken in their sails; restore her to her father's arms, and he will embrace you, too.

Leander. And you—?

Harlequin. —follow the wind in the tree-tops. Marry your Columbine; you two will be as happy as it is in human nature to be. Are we friends?

Leander. Friends! [*They embrace.*]

Harlequin. There is day.

Leander. And with day comes love.

Enter Columbine, *R.*

Columbine. Leander!

Harlequin. Searching all night, dying of distress. You owe him for this—what?

Columbine. I—I do not know.

Harlequin. I think you do. Now you had better set out before others wake.

Columbine. That fierce, beautiful woman! Farewell.

Harlequin [*kissing her hand*]. My dear, your loveliness will never leave me.

Columbine's Marriage

Enter FLOWER-DE-LUCE, *L.*

Flower-de-Luce. Ah!
Harlequin. Be off. [*Exeunt* COLUMBINE *and*
LEANDER, *R.*] Softly, my dear, softly. I'll gladly do
the same by you. [*Embraces her.*]

Enter PIERROT, *L.*

Pierrot. Ho! ho! What do these eyes see?
Flower-de-Luce. A fist, fool.
[*Strikes him and exit, R.*

Enter CAPTAIN BRAZENNOSE *and* DR. WISEMAN.

Captain Brazennose [*whom* FLOWER-DE-LUCE *has
jostled*]. She's a stunning ghost. I'm sorry I did
not stay up. What, more ghosts? My visit, good
host, if unexpected, is less of an intrusion than an
honour, for I am the renowned Captain Brazennose,
and this is my dearest friend, the distinguished Dr.
Wiseman.
Dr. Wiseman. As great in the arts of peace as
my friend there in those military, martial, specifically
bellicose. My province is all knowledge.
Pierrot. On my soul, they are so blinded with
gazing on their glorious selves that they cannot see

us. Captain, you have not forgotten your second of the morning? Doctor —

Dr. Wiseman. Come away, Captain Brazennose; come, come, come, which is to say thrice quick. They will set us again at combat and peace is my province. [*Exit with* Captain Brazennose, *R.*

Harlequin. So, Pierrot, we are where we were, alone, and a new day begun. Hear the winds call us. [*Sings.*]

> The wind blows out of the door of day,
> The pine trees toss to point the way,
> And the long white road runs over and on
> Whither the souls of the dead are gone;
> Dead feet patter, dead voices say,
> "Over the hills and far away."

[*Exeunt, L.*

CURTAIN

THE MAGIC HAT

PUPPETS

MERCHANT, *Lucilla's father.*	Dress of a soldier, sword in hand, large cocked hat.
DON ALONZO, *the unwelcome lover.*	Similar dress, a stick in his hand.
LEANDER, *Lucilla's lover.*	Court dress, sword in hand.
SANDRO, *a poet.*	The same.
TONY, *Leander's servant.*	Harlequin.
TOBY, *father's servant.*	Harlequin.
CLOWN, *Don Alonzo's servant.*	
SERVANT, *to the father.*	Clown's dress.
LUCILLA, *the Merchant's daughter.*	Court dress, fan in hand.
LAURETTA, *his niece.*	The same.
MARIANNA, *waiting-woman.*	Short skirt, apron, and cap.

Properties: a lute, an extra cocked hat.

The Magic Hat

ACT I

S<small>CENE</small>: *A Public Place. Church at back.*

Enter, R., L<small>UCILLA</small> *and* L<small>AURETTA</small>, *followed by* M<small>ARIANNA</small>; *they cross over and exeunt, L.*

Enter L<small>EANDER</small> *and* T<small>ONY</small>.

Tony. Master, master, she went this way.

Leander. No, this way.

Tony. In short, master, having made an appointment secretly with her lover, she goes to church to justify it.

Leander. Her father's cruel persecution of our love would justify worse acts than saying her prayers.

Tony. And indeed the church is one of the two

95

places where she is certain not to meet your rival and her father's choice, Don Alonzo.

Leander. What is the other? Let me know that I may look elsewhere; for I would rather, I think, see him than even my dearest Lucilla — if it were alone, and where I could treat him according to his deserts.

Tony. Faith, the other is the field of combat, in spite of his soldier finery. But if you wait for Don Alonzo's deserts, and put off your affair with Mistress Lucilla till he has them, you must go unmarried to your grave, for he deserves nothing.

Leander. And so, please you, I shall wait for nothing.

Enter SANDRO, *R., singing.*

I follow Beauty over earth
  And under sea;
The fairies gave her at my birth
  For bride to me.

The fairies gave me at my birth
  A wandering will,
A lonely heart, that all the girth
  O' the world can't fill.

The fairies gave, to set me free
  From change and time,
The heart to feel, the eye to see,
  The lips of rhyme.

"I follow Beauty over earth and under sea."

The Magic Hat

[*Speaks.*] I know she passed here, for as I came by yonder garden wall a bird was singing, so I stopped to sing to him again and perhaps missed her. Leander! This is a fortunate meeting. Has any one passed since you were here?

Leander. No one, Sandro, whom you could be in search of. But how long have you been at home? I thought I left you under an almond tree counting the pink blossoms as they fell.

Sandro. Not so fast; that was last week. There are cheeks pinker than the delicate almond flowers, and feet that touch the earth more lightly than the frail fluttering petals. Come, I know she passed this way, for the smell of almonds is in the air. Let me follow, dear Leander. [*Going, L.*]

Tony. Faith, master, don't let him go an inch or I swear he will take an ell.

Leander. O Sandro, Sandro, are you false to me? You love her? Then defend yourself! [*Raises his arm.* SANDRO *does the same, but* TONY *throws himself between.*]

Tony. Get back, put up your swords. Here comes the authorized lover. You, Master Sandro, go into church awhile; my own good lord must get away to the transept door, for she will be coming soon, while I watch. Any time will do for fighting, but now there is business on hand.

[*Exeunt* SANDRO, *R.*, LEANDER *and* TONY, *L.*

Enter DON ALONZO, *beating* CLOWN.

Clown. Truly, master, 'tis not my fault if I have no better message. Heaven has been good to me, sir, in that it has given me a stout back to stand drubbing, since it has withheld the wit to frame lies. Your mere truth-teller, sir, like myself, is a simple fellow.

Don Alonzo. Enough, fool! Say your message again.

Clown. That I may be beaten again? No, I have had enough already.

Don Alonzo. Repeat the girl's words, I say.

Clown. My mistress says, quoth Marianna, that she will never willingly see his ugly face again. [DON ALONZO *raises his arm.*] It was not I called it ugly; I hope I have too much wit to call your face ugly to your face, master. Now I am all out. Where was I? "I cannot forbid him my father's house," said she; "but when he comes into a room, I shall go out of it." So far the lady. But, master, there is more which you should have heard an hour ago had you not beat me so hastily. Now, if you like the tale better, then is the beating undeserved and so wasted — as the saying is, haste makes waste. When I had Marianna in the kitchen and had given her the purse: "Truly," said she, "it might have been heavier, but it jingles not amiss. If he had not such an ugly face" — master, if you beat me we shall never get on. Then she bit her lip awhile in thought, muttering. Lastly she cried out, "I have it!"

Don Alonzo. Well, what had she?

Clown. Well, sir, she had the money. And she gave me something for you, moreover, a cocked hat, much such to look at as you have on at this moment and none too clean nor new; but looks are not to be trusted, and an ugly face *may* cover a good heart, as my old mother used to say to me. So this hat, which is almost as your own, is one of the family treasures, and my fair Mistress Lucilla stole it out of the great painted chest, that Master Leander might visit her unseen in the garden. "For," said Marianna, "whoever wears it is invisible; bid your master clap it on and come wooing of my mistress; she will take him for Leander, and I warrant he will find her more of a coming-on disposition."

Don Alonzo. But the hat, fool, the hat!

Clown. Safe at home, master, under lock and key; do but return to fetch it, then seek Lucilla in the garden. [*Exeunt, R.*

Enter, L., LUCILLA, LAURETTA, *and* MARIANNA, *followed by* LEANDER *and* TONY. MARIANNA *loiters.* *Exeunt* LUCILLA *and* LAURETTA.

Tony. Here is Marianna ready to tell us if the plan I just unfolded to you has succeeded, and you shall have your revenge on Don Alonzo sooner than you looked for. Well, Mistress Mischief, has the fish bit?

Marianna. He is safely hooked, saving your presence, good Master Leander; for the clown has gone off to the braggart with my master's second best hat, and presently you shall see him as fantastic as a blind man in company.

Leander. But when the servant sees his master put on the hat without disappearing, the game is up.

Marianna. That he shall not see, for I will carry him off with me, and you shall behold Don Alonzo persuaded that he is invisible.

The Magic Hat

Leander. There is hope in this, and you shall not find me ungrateful.

Tony. O rare jest! My gratitude comes later, but comes surely. [*Exit* MARIANNA, *R.*] O golden minx!

[*Exeunt, L.*

CURTAIN

ACT II

SCENE: *A Garden Wall and Practicable Gate, L. Arbour or Bush, R.*

Enter, R., LAURETTA, *then* LUCILLA.

Lucilla. My sweet cousin, you have not laughed above three times to-day, and just now you threw down your embroidery with a great sigh and stole away here. I am afraid — are you not ill?

Lauretta. O my little, pretty, sweet coz, it is a catching sickness. Your care for me comes too late. I think I must have — caught it from you.

Lucilla. Now, by your love for me, explain yourself.

Lauretta. Now by yours for me, which is I know unchanged, and yet has dwindled in comparison till it is like a star when the moon is up, I see no need for explanation.

The Magic Hat

Lucilla. I cannot follow you. Are you not my cousin and dearest friend?

Lauretta. No, it is I who follow you along the way of dear unrest and troublesome delight. As truly as you are my cousin, so am I not your dearest friend — say I truth, littlest, prettiest, sweetest friend of Leander? But, soberly, coz, I cannot be happy while you trick your father.

Lucilla. Nor can I, alas! And yet it is the only way to keep Leander from despair.

Lauretta. He is to come here presently while your father is from home, is he not?

Lucilla. Yes, but only that I may tell him he must not come. Surely in time my father will dismiss this Spaniard, who alone stands between me and all I love — father, you, Leander. But are you really in love? Is it not a blessed state?

Lauretta. Troth, cousin, not as the old Kindergartner Plato describes that, for thence were poets banished. Of all countries it is most like England, for my little kingdom from being swayed by a woman's will on a sudden finds itself with a new ruler, and that in the image of a man.

Lucilla. Is it possible that you love my Leander's dear Sandro? But you must set a guard over your tongue, for not even to him has Leander spoken of his suit.

Lauretta. For fear Sandro should follow suit? Then we were all well suited.

Lucilla. Be sober a moment and tell me it is he.

Lauretta. Oh, I am mad with new delight. If it is not Sandro, then certainly it is a falling star, for I found him shining under an almond tree. So, like Robin Redbreast, I covered him up with the rosy leaves.

Enter, outside the gate, Don Alonzo.

Lucilla. Hush! here some one comes. I should know his step. Oh, it is Don Alonzo!—and Leander soon to come! In, in quickly before he sees us, and let us think what to do.

Lauretta. With all thinking and no doing Clytie grew into the flower that still wags her heavy head so foolishly. [*Exeunt, R.*

Don Alonzo [*through the gate*]. The hat is a little small, certainly, but it fits the tighter for that. My servant is gone of an errand for Marianna before I could ask him if it became me. But of course he could not have seen. The girl tells me her mistress is alone in the arbour, now will I woo her softly. [*Tries the gate.*] Holà, where is the key? Good cheer, Captain, you have climbed many a wall to get out of the way of danger, now prove the strength of your vaulting ambition. [*Jumps over the wall.*] So! [*Advancing softly.*] My Lady Lucilla, be not affrighted when you see this disembodied voice, for it has the rapture of beholding unclouded your charms. Did not Jove woo in a shower of gold and Dan Phœbus in — in — oh, in what? — in a shower of rain, perhaps. Hey! there's no one here. Now have I wasted all the sweet speech which I stole out of Sandro the poet's pocket as he came home from church this morning.

Enter, outside, LEANDER *and* TONY.

Tony. There he stands, like a gutter spout in dry weather, gaping for occupation. Now if your wit cannot make his folly the occasion of revenge, I will serve you no more; for folly is catching, and I would not make the third.

Leander. Peace, he will hear. [*Unlocking the gate.*] Now, Tony, since we are alone, tell me what Marianna said to you.

Tony. Only, sir [did you see him turn?], that her master thought of the Spanish Captain's pocket and brains equally ill, both being a vacuum, which nature

MEMORIE

...ch : ...

...NO: NOT

...get s

DELL...

Laurell

makes

death

AL

Striking

so much

fact.

reach

ALONZO

"Oh, Oh! Ah, ah! I must cry out. Oh, Oh!"

abhors; that he is marrying Mistress Lucilla to him from pure unnatural spite, that he may afterward cast her off and make Lauretta his heiress. [Note how he started, sir.]

Leander. I cannot believe that he would deal so with his only child.

Tony. Oh, sir, she is a vixen; you had better let her go and court her merry cousin, Mistress Lauretta.

Leander. Do you speak rudely of my mistress, rascal? [*Starts to beat him;* TONY *dodges behind* DON ALONZO, *who gets the blows.*]

Don Alonzo [*suppressing his cries*]. Oh, oh! Ah, ah! I must cry out. Oh, oh!

Tony. Cool yourself, master, you are only striking empty air. Take my word for it, Lauretta is as much the sweeter in temper as she is the fairer in face.

Leander. Knave, scoundrel, villain, I will reach you yet! [*Same business as before.* DON ALONZO *tries vainly to get from between them.*]

Tony. Hark! do I not hear voices?

Enter LUCILLA, *R.*

Leander [*going hastily to entrance and meeting her; aside to her*]. That wretched intruder believes himself invisible; consent, in order to punish him, to act

"Oh, Oh! Ah, ah! I must cry out. Oh, Oh!"

as though he were. [*Aloud*.] Lady of my life, at last I see you alone. [*To* TONY.] Off, fellow, and watch the gate. [*To* LUCILLA.] I kiss your hand and lay my heart before your feet.

Don Alonzo. Oh, that I were in her place to stamp on it!

Lucilla. Dear Leander!

Don Alonzo. Rascal Leander!

Leander. When I think of you exposed to the odious courtship of that importunate coward, I could go mad. Tell me again that you detest him.

Lucilla. He is as distasteful to me as you are delightful.

Don Alonzo. I will wring his neck for this.

[*Going toward them.*

Tony [*running up and kicking him away*]. Ouch! Pardon, sir, I have to warn you that twilight is coming on and I stubbed my foot against a stone somewhere here. [*Kicking* DON ALONZO.] There it is again. Lend me your sword, master, to knock it away.

[DON ALONZO *runs out,* TONY *resumes his former place by the gate, peeping around the corner.*

Lucilla. Dear Leander, Lauretta and I have serious things to say to you.

[*Exeunt* LEANDER *and* LUCILLA, *R.*

Enter SANDRO, *L., lute in hand.*

Sandro. These nights the moon, like a faithful nun, is up and at watch before the sun is well gone. The nightingale began an hour ago; I cannot keep silence longer. [*Sings.*]

> I follow Beauty, over earth
> > Or under sea;
> And all the light-foot brood of Mirth
> > Once followed me.

> I follow Beauty, so thine eyes
> > Yet lead me on —
> Alone, now, for as daylight dies
> > Even Laughter's gone.

Enter LEANDER, *R.*

Leander. Who is in this garden? What robber dares —?   [*Hurries off, L.*

Sandro. I am here.   [*Follows, L.*

Tony. Oh, my master will certainly kill him!
        [*Exit L.*

Enter LUCILLA *and* LAURETTA, *R.*

Lucilla. This way they went. I heard their voices. Oh, Leander is dangerous!

Lauretta. I do not fear for Sandro, but for Leander when he knows the singer. We must follow.

Lucilla. They are in the myrtle thicket.

[*Exeunt, L.*

Enter LEANDER, SANDRO *following, L.*

Leander [*turns*]. O faithless, faithless friend! Draw and defend yourself.

Sandro. Alas, Leander, I have only my lute, and you could not strike that guiltless servant. Why should you be angry with me? I have not spoken once since to her. You would not stop my singing?

Enter LUCILLA *and* LAURETTA, *L.*

Both. Leander!

Enter MARIANNA, *R.*

Marianna. Mistresses both, make haste indoors, here is master home. Come, come, before he misses you! [*Exit, R.*

Lucilla. Oh, farewell, my dear love. Make haste away.

Lauretta. His anger with us — the danger to you — go, go! [*Exeunt* LUCILLA *and* LAURETTA, *R.*

H 113

Enter TONY, *R.*

Tony. For sweet charity's sake, Master Sandro, get you gone in the shadow. My master is entirely mad. He knows no more what he does than do those two pretty, frightened children who are maidenly mad, or yourself, saving your poetship, who are, I take it, musically mad, or the Spanish captain who is stark mad, or even Marianna and myself who are but mischievously mad. Adieu, sir; let us go pray for a change in the moon.

[*Exit* SANDRO, *L., followed by* TONY *and then by* LEANDER.

CURTAIN

ACT III

SCENE: *A Room in the Merchant's House.*

Enter MARIANNA, *L., meeting* TOBY, *R.*

Marianna [*starts and screams*].

Toby. It is I, sister.

Marianna. Who was it called you just now?

Toby. Our master. The Spanish Captain is with him.

Marianna. Then all is up with us.

Toby. Very like; you should not have got into scrapes when I was not here to get you out.

Marianna. Since you are here, now, and I have just told you everything, suppose your wisdom proceeds to get us all out.

Toby. "Brother," said the fly in the molasses jug, "come pull me up." There is but one device, for the Captain is, unlike most Spaniards, a most notorious coward.

Marianna. I will send his servant from below to call him hither.   [*Exit, L.*

Toby. Now, Toby, spur thy wit. Alas! it has been hard ridden. That man should get him a wit of india-rubber enclosed in a brain of adamant, who would serve a choleric old gentleman and three pretty girls.

Enter MARIANNA, *L.*

Marianna. Quick, brother! I sent the gentleman word that Mistress Lucilla called him.

Enter DON ALONZO, *and* CLOWN, *R.*

Don Alonzo. Madam, your commands — here is no lady. Fool!   [*Exit* MARIANNA, *L.*

Clown. She said so — now is she gone, too. I think we shall presently all appear and vanish instead of using the door, and it will be a great saving of shoe leather.

Don Alonzo. You have lied to me! [*Beating him over the head.*]

The Magic Hat

Clown. Who? I, sir? No, sir! I never lie. Truly, you could not expect a liar when you pay only a crown a week — and this week it is a crown with a hole in it. [*Exit, L.*

Toby. As you said truly, sir, here is no lady fool, nor no foolish lady neither. You will not again see my young mistress.

Don Alonzo. But Mistress Lauretta, I should like to see her.

Toby. No more than the other.

Don Alonzo. I do not ask to see the other, since I now know I shall not see her inheritance.

Toby. Softly, sir, there are more words to that. Have you told my master of your changed affection?

Don Alonzo. Ah — no — I thought I should tell the lady first.

Toby. A wise conclusion, sir, for you would not have told her afterward.

Don Alonzo. How so?

Toby. Because, sir, dead men tell no tales.

Don Alonzo. But this will never do! What shall I do?

Toby. This, sir. Tell her father that your late story was all a device to try his mind toward you;

that Mistress Lucilla is on-coming, Master Leander reasonably disposed, Marianna civil, and your servant yonder a clever fellow; restore the magic hat and withdraw to your inn for the night. Thence you may take horse for your own country, where the women, if less witty, are more wealthy; if less fair, are more favourable. I will light you to him.

[*Exeunt, R.*

Enter SANDRO, *L.,* SERVANT *ushering him.*

Servant. This way, sir. I will tell my lady.

[*Exit, R.*

Sandro. My spirit, like a miser's, still wanders about the spot where its treasure lies. I had a good thought this morning for a serenade, but the paper must have fallen from my pocket. Let me see — let me see —

[*Stands aside.*

Enter MERCHANT *and* DON ALONZO.

Merchant. This is a strange business, Don Alonzo. I scarcely know how to take it. And that hat of yours I mightily mistrust, for though there is a legend in the family of such a magical inheritance, yet this has not been seen for upward of two hundred years.

The Magic Hat

Don Alonzo. It is no doubt one of your ancestors', for it smells of sulphur and brimstone — I mean,
it has a somewhat mouldy savour, and fumigation
with sulphur would be good.

Merchant. Do I understand you wish to restore
the hat to me?

Don Alonzo. Assuredly. I have no use for it —
further. Since I am much fatigued with the day's
exercise, I have the honour to wish you a very good
night.

Merchant. Good night to you, Don Alonzo, and
good repose.

Don Alonzo. A mind at ease is the best repose,
and that I hope to enjoy.

Merchant. Farewell till to-morrow. Toby, light
the gentleman.

Don Alonzo. Till the Day of Judgment — I am
yours, sir. Absence will only endear you.

[*Exit after* TOBY, *L.*

Merchant. Marianna!

Enter MARIANNA, *L.*

Request your mistresses. [*Exit* MARIANNA, *R.*

Enter Toby, *L.*

You, sir, do you know of this hat?

Toby. I have heard of it, sir.

Merchant. You believe?

Toby. Sir, they say we must believe or suffer eternally.

Merchant. Good. We will try now whether my stick can discern your back.

Toby. Oh, sir, press not belief too hard. I am not the stuff of which martyrs are made.

Merchant. Do not dispute, sirrah! Go fetch it from the hall; you are under my eyes.

> [*Exit* Toby; *returns in hat. The* Merchant *chases him about the stage; they stumble on* Sandro. *Exit* Toby, *R.*

Holà! who's this?

Toby [*reëntering without the hat*]. A strange wild-fowl, master, a marketer of metres, a fashioner of phrases, a sort of hostage to posterity for all of us. We must be beholden to him in the long run, but just now he would, I estimate, as lief be beholden to you for a short span — the hand of Mistress Lauretta, your niece.

The Magic Hat

Enter LUCILLA *and* LAURETTA, *R.*

Sandro. The rascal for once speaks half a truth, sir. I love that lady all too well, but I am not her suitor.

Merchant. How, Master Sandro, do you scorn my niece?

Sandro. Never. I reverence her infinitely, but my love is not mine, but my dear Leander's. For me, love is enough.

Merchant. Leander fickle? You see now, daughter, for whom you have disobeyed your father and disdained an honourable captain.

Lucilla. O unhappy Lucilla!

Lauretta. Nay, uncle, if Leander loves me, he is the best dissembler in Italy. Cousin, cousin, if he has no more credit than that, what will you go to housekeeping on? Look up, smile, we'll ask him; and here he comes.

Enter LEANDER, *L.*

Leander. News, great news! Dearest, best Lucilla, be glad with me. Pardon, sir her father; you have forbid me the house, but I come to tell you that the Spaniard has fled the town. Perhaps your man, Toby, can tell you more at a fitting time. Meanwhile, may not our mutual constancy, our steadfast affection, find a reward at last?

Merchant. Leander, had you spoken thus openly before, you might have found me kindlier. My daughter has this night confessed and been forgiven, and not to punish her I must forgive you, too — unless the poet's tale —

Leander. O my poor Sandro, had I seen you before, I would have spared you the sad success of my happier love. We both have striven, but the prize is for me alone.

Sandro. I am in a maze. Do you not love Lauretta?

Leander. Do you not love Lucilla?

Merchant. This is a happy ending. Niece, lend me your hand a moment, that I may bestow it on Sandro.

Lauretta. Not so fast, uncle. How do you know I want to be so generous with my appendages? You would not have a left-handed niece?

Sandro. Lauretta, it is impossible that I should love so mightily were not your love a part.

Lauretta. You are right, my poet; but I say

with you, love is enough. More were superfluity. We will think on one another six days in the week, and you shall come and sing to me o' Sundays.

Merchant. Have patience, Sandro, with this wild girl; when she sees Lucilla married, her turn will come.

Sandro. Perhaps you are right, Lauretta, perhaps you are. How I will sing!

Enter SERVANT, *R.*

Servant. Supper waits, master, and has waited so long it must be very tired. [*Exit, R.*

Merchant. Come in, son and nephew, come in, my girls.

Enter TONY, MARIANNA, *and* TOBY, *L.*

Tony. One moment, by your favour; there is another match to be made. I am promised to this Marianna, sir, whenever she should bring my master's suit to a happy end, and here is Toby to remind us of it.

Merchant. Tony and Marianna, mischievous both, I can devise no better punishment than to bind you to each other. To-morrow I will see you married,

Comedies and Legends for Marionettes

and your wedding gift shall be the magic hat, but let me never see you after.   Music, ho! and let us dance. [*Dance.*]

CURTAIN

LEGENDS

THE LEGEND OF S. FRANCIS

PUPPETS

S. FRANCIS.	Court dress in Act I, then gray frock, with girdle of knotted rope.
PIETRO BERNARDONE, *his father*.	Merchant's dress.
THE BISHOP OF ASSISI.	Cope, mitre, pastoral staff, gloves, chain with cross.
PRIEST OF S. DAMIAN'S.	Black frock, shovel hat.
BROTHER BERNARD	
BROTHER LEO	*followers of*
BROTHER JUNIPER	*S. Francis.* Gray frocks, knotted girdles.
A YOUNG BROTHER	
PACIFICO, *a companion of S. Francis.*	Court dress.
ANOTHER COMPANION.	The same.
THE BAILIFF OF ASSISI.	Merchant's dress, gold chain.
CLOWN, *Pietro Bernardone's servant.*	Blue smock frock, white trousers.
GIAN, *an old man.*	
PICA, *S. Francis's mother.*	Black dress, white coif.
S. CLARE.	Court dress, chains on neck, girdle, rings, and bracelets.
AGNES, *a little girl.*	
VANNA, *Gian's wife.*	Peasant's dress.
WOLF.	
BIRDS.	
TOWNSPEOPLE.	

Properties: a sack, a bag of money, a looking-glass, a pipe, an axe, a spade.

The Legend of S. Francis

ACT I

OF HIS CALLING

SCENE: *Outside his Father's House. Night. During the Early Part of the Scene Light grows brighter.*

Enter GIAN, R., *carrying a sack.*

Gian. Oh, oh! my poor old back! Now if Master Francis saw me doubled up with a heavy load, he'd take half of it. But there he is in yonder, in his broadcloth and scarlet. Oh, he is a comely boy, and the fashions are pretty fashions upon him, and his smile is a gentle smile, and he can sing so that a man forgets he's old and hungry and cold o' the winter nights. But he is singing and dancing, eating and drinking, till the sun will be up before he is abed. Well, well, I was up betimes to work, so work I must.
[*Exit, L.*

Enter S. FRANCIS *and* TWO COMPANIONS, *L.*

S. Francis.   So hot it was in there, and here the air is still and cool, and how the stars are calm!

Pacifico.   What is the matter now, Francis?

2d Companion.   Oh, let him alone, he is hunting for a wife in the stars.

S. Francis.   True; for a fairer wife than you could fancy ever.   [*Sings.*]

> The wind that blew across my brow
>   Is almost gone;
> The golden stars grow paler now
>   Before the dawn.
>
> One star there in its radiant place
>   Undimmed yet gleams,
> And I — I brood upon a face
>   More fair than dreams.

Pacifico.   Francis, they call me the King of Verse and the Courtly Doctor of Singers, but —

S. Francis [*dreamily*].   Perhaps they will call me God's Minstrel.

2d Companion.   Come on, he has been getting madder and madder this year past.   I'll go home and go to bed.   [*Exeunt* COMPANIONS, *R.*

The Legend of S. Francis

S. Francis. Certainly this year past I have been strange even to myself. I try to be good and kind to people, and loving, but for me there is not anywhere any peace. Perhaps when I have rebuilt the poor little church of S. Damian's, I shall be at rest, and that will I do, though I should have to carry the stones on my back and lay them with my own hands. [*Pause.*] The sun is up, that most beautiful creature of the whole creation.

Enter PRIEST, *R., with a bag.*

Good morning, father.

Priest. Good morning, my son. I cannot understand about this great bag of gold you left with me yesterday. ·

S. Francis. It is for building the church.

Priest. Where did you find so much?

S. Francis. I took four bales of my father's stuff and sold them. I dare say he will be angry when he finds out.

Priest. But that was wrong.

S. Francis. But, father, it was the only way I could get any money at all. My father will give me none. This great feast last night was for my birthday; he gave it, not I. Oh, I think of the poor little church, how it is tumbling down.

Priest. I must have clean money to build with. This stolen gold would flame out between the bricks. Take your pelf. [*Exit, R.*

S. Francis. Oh, what can I do?

Enter Pietro Bernardone, *L.*

Pietro Bernardone [*very angry*]. What's this I hear from Foligno of your selling cloth?

S. Francis. It is quite so, sir. I sold the cloth to get money to rebuild S. Damian's.

Pietro Bernardone. Then you're a thief, and to be treated as such. [*Beats him.*] I must lock you up. [*Exit with* S. Francis.

Reënter, L., with Clown.

Here, Peter, look after that boy of mine while I am gone. I have to hurry to Foligno to see about the business there; he has not even the sense left to drive a good bargain. [*Exit, R.*

Clown. I'll tell you what, he can drive a horse. You should have seen him on the road to Foligno. Gee — up! Woah! Houp-là! Look out that the big gray wolf does not eat you, master. He'd die of indigestion, sure, you're such a tough mouthful, and peppery, too — then we'd be rid of two bad things at one gulp, so to speak.

Enter S. FRANCIS *and* PICA, *L.*

Pica. Dear boy, your father is justly angered with you; but, Francis, I cannot see you suffer. Go to the good priest of S. Damian's and Heaven keep you.

Clown. Hola! my master must know this. They say ill news travels fast enough; but I think it would scarcely get to him soon enough without my legs.

[*Exit, R.*

S. Francis. If I go, dearest mother, I shall not come home again. But I obey you. Ah, mother — [*Embraces her.*]   [*Exeunt, L. and R.*

Enter PIETRO BERNARDONE *with the* BAILIFF, *R.*

Bailiff. My good friend, my excellent master merchant, I had not done breakfast, and Justice looks asquint when she is hungry; but out of the fulness of the mouth the heart speaketh.

Pietro Bernardone. Justice, Master Bailiff, is not a thing of times and seasons.

Bailiff. There is a time for all things, and this was breakfast time. Moreover, I see no offender. Bethink you, Master Bernardone, he is your own flesh and blood — a little lamb chop of yours, so to speak, a spare rib out of your side of bacon, which would go well dished up with a trim little green cabbage of a girl.

Pietro Bernardone. With a green goose! No son of mine, from now on. [*Walking to wings, R., and looking.*] Here is Peter bringing him.

Enter S. Francis *and* Clown, *R.*

S. Francis. You sent, sir, for me.

Pietro Bernardone. This magistrate will settle with you.

Clown. And that, shortly, or he's not so hungry as my master thinks him.

S. Francis. Sir, I have cast in my lot with the Church, the civil power can lay no hand on me.

Bailiff. Humph! you might have let me finish my breakfast.   [*Exit, R.*

Clown. A very uncivil power this morning.

Pietro Bernardone. I guessed this — you may wait for the Bishop.

Enter Bishop, *R.*

My lord, this son of mine has stolen my gold and disobeyed my commands.

The Legend of S. Francis

S. Francis.   Father and lord, I took it for the
Church because that man would give me none.

Pietro Bernardone.   You know that I give, sir, to
the Church generously.   Shall that madman reduce
us all to poverty?

Bishop.   I have heard of this already from the
priest.   Francis, restore the gold; for what comes
wrongfully is not for holy use.   Have faith, my boy
— act like a man.

S. Francis.   If I were idle, if I were extravagant,
if I were wicked even, my father would not let me
lack.   Here is his gold [*throwing it down*], here is
his scarlet cloth [*taking off his cloak*] — all that was
his I give back to him.

Enter GIAN, *L.*

Old man, lend me your coat that I may have something in my poverty to cover myself withal.   [*Exit, L.*

Gian.   Lackaday, Master Francis, what does the
likes of you talking of poverty to the likes of me?

[*Exit, L.*

Pietro Bernardone.   O my lord, the ungrateful
son!   Never was boy loved as I have loved him.
[*Weeps.*]   His mother named him John, but his baby
name was my little Frenchman, my Francis.

Comedies and Legends for Marionettes

Bishop.   Peace, Bernardone; you have chosen to withstand the heavenly grace working in your son, and your portion will be sorrow.   Francis shall be a holy man.

Enter S. FRANCIS, *L.*, *in* GIAN'S *smock.*

Pietro Bernardone.   That is not my son.   My son is dead.

S. Francis.   I have no human father.   Farewell, I go to seek my bride.

Bishop.   Marriage, Francis?

S. Francis.   Yes, my lord — to Poverty.

CURTAIN

ACT II

OF HIS CALLING OTHERS

Scene: *A Public Square, the Church behind.*

Enter, L., Gian *and* Brother Bernard.

Gian. By your favor, and no offence, master.

Brother Bernard. Brother, you mean, Gian.

Gian. It is not for the likes of me to call the likes of you brother.

Brother Bernard. Oh, dear heart, we be all brothers.

Gian. Well, well. I have heard tell of one old grandfather, Adam; but I reckoned the gentlefolk did not count cousins so far, let alone brothers. Well, well, you were the first to go about with Master

Francis, were you not? Do you mind the day when all the folk stoned him here in Assisi? Alas! that I should have lived to see that day. I said to my wife Vanna, said I —

Brother Bernard. You had a question to ask me, had not you?

Gian. Yes, yes. When you and he were in that huge wonderful city of Rome, what did you do? There is a deal of talk about some dream or other; for my part, I do not hold much with dreams.

Brother Bernard. Some dreams are holy. The Pope himself dreamed that that great church of S. John Lateran was falling down, and that men came to prop it with their shoulders. One was the very learned Spaniard Dominic, and who do you think was the other?

Gian. Even Francis? Little Master Francis that I used to carry about in these arms? Welladay! welladay! They tell me he is to preach this afternoon. [*Exeunt, R.*

Enter S. FRANCIS *and the* WOLF.

S. Francis. Come here, Brother Wolf. You were going to eat me up, but I commanded you by the Most Holy Name to do no harm, and you lay down gently as a dog. Now I am going to talk to you. Know you not that you are a thief and a base murderer, and that all the men in this countryside do hate you? And that is terrible. Therefore I must make peace between you and them, and because some of your wickedness came of your being hungry, you shall never be hungry again, but if you go to people's doors, they will give you something always to eat. And you must be gentle and kind, and the friend of all the world. Do you promise me that? [WOLF *nods.*] Then give me your right paw for a pledge. [WOLF *does so.*]   [*Exit* WOLF, *R.*

Enter a YOUNG BROTHER, *L.*

Young Brother. I can read a little, Brother Francis; may not I have a psalter of my own that I can sing psalms out of in the choir?

S. Francis. Have you not asked me this before?

Young Brother. Yes, Brother Francis.

S. Francis. Now look you: if I let you have a psalter, you will be wanting next thing a breviary; and when you have a breviary, then you will be sitting up in your stall like a lordly bishop and saying to one of your brothers, "Brother, fetch me my breviary."   [*Exeunt, R.*

Enter, R., a number of people and pass across the stage. Lastly enter S. CLARE *and* AGNES, *followed by* PACIFICO, *who remains half in the wings, watching.*

Agnes. Dear Clare, why are you in silk and satin to-day, with all your jewels on? I thought it was wrong to spend time adorning oneself.

S. Clare. Sweet sister, it is right to obey mamma, and she bade me make myself gay for this great feast.

Agnes. Sister, I never saw you look so beautiful.

S. Clare. Agnes, if my soul was beautiful, then only might I be worth looking at.

[*Exeunt* S. CLARE *and* AGNES, *L.*

Enter S. FRANCIS, BROTHER BERNARD, *and* GIAN, *R.*

Brother Bernard. Brother, it is time for your sermon, but the swallows wheeling up above the church make such a noise that nobody will be able to hear you.

S. Francis. Little sisters, you swallows up there, you must hold your peace now, for it is my turn to speak and to sing.

[*Exit, L., with* BROTHER BERNARD.

Gian. Why, 'tis as still as on the hottest days at noon, when you hear the timbers in the roof

140

stretching themselves for heat. There goes Master Francis to the pulpit. I shall never teach my poor old tongue new tricks. I must hobble along after, lest I lose one word out of his blessed lips. Where's my wife? Vanna, I say! Vanna! [*Exit, L.*

Pacifico. Again the beautiful girl! I saw her in church this morning; she was too shy and modest to go up to the altar with the rest of us for a palm, and the Bishop himself carried one down to where she stood in her place. Now is she listening [*looks out, L.*] to my old friend Francis. Hey, Brother Bernard!

Enter BROTHER BERNARD, *L.*

I want to ask you an honest question. This same Francis of yours, — he used to be mine, yours and mine, and everybody's Francis, — I hear, has converted the Soldan of Egypt. But how is he at home, in S. Mary of the Little Portion? I have always doubted whether a man that loves the whole world be a good next-door neighbour.

Brother Bernard. Messire, he is the gentlest soul alive, and the most loving and tender. A hare pursued by a greyhound leaped into his bosom, and he saved the frightened thing.

Pacifico. That does not answer me, for I have always thought that any one who would sit up with a sick cat was not likely to sit up with a sick person.

Brother Bernard. Indeed, Master Pacifico, I think that he who would not sit up with a sick creature would not be apt to sit up, neither, with a sick servant.

Pacifico. One more question. When men dwell so much on the love of heaven, they have sometimes a very special corner for the love of earth. This Brother of yours, who has given up father and mother for the Religion — are you sure he is not writing songs to some bright lady?

Brother Bernard. Indeed, friend, Brother Francis makes much pretty praise of his most sweet lady. If you will come some night into the little wood close by Our Lady of the Little Portion, you may hear him singing.

Pacifico. You are a good fellow. I'll come sure.

[*Exit, R., exit* Brother Bernard, *L.*

Enter Gian, *R., meeting* Vanna, *L.*

Gian. Eh, Vanna, that was a wonderful preaching! Certainly we must forsake all our vanities and vices.

"The miserable thing was throwing my pipe away."

The Legend of S. Francis

Vanna. Why, so say I too, and throw them into the river lest we slide back again.

Gian. Just my thought, so here I am going — and you have a bundle, too.

Vanna. Eh, eh, Gian, what's that you're carrying?

Gian. What, but your looking-glass, my precious old woman, for the good of your immortal soul. You would not miss seeing the blessed angels through staring at your own poor perishing face?

Vanna. Heard ever any one the like? You might just let my superfluities alone, old man, and think of your own shortcomings.

Gian. I'll be bound you thought of them enough for two. What's that in your hand? Hold it out, old woman. Oh, oh, my precious pipe! How dare you touch it! [*Beats her till she runs off, R.*]

Enter S. Francis.

S. Francis. What is this noise? Why, my good old friend, what is the trouble with your poor wife?

Gian. The miserable thing was throwing my pipe away.

S. Francis. What, what, what? Where is all the peace of this blessed day? Where is the gentleness and love you promised to all the world just now?

Oh, Gian, are you going to let a miserable clay pipe lead you into sin this way? Smoking seemed no great harm before, but you see after all the devil was there.

Gian [*weeping*]. O blessed Francis, forgive me and pray for my forgiveness. I will never smoke again. Vanna, my old woman —

S. Francis. There's my good brother!

[*Exit* GIAN, *R.*

Now is my brother Sun very tired and hurrying home. It grows cold!

Enter S. CLARE, *L.*

S. Clare. O Brother Francis, I cannot longer withstand my own heart and the voice that cries in it and will not cease. Open for me your holy order, take away all these silks and jewels that weigh me down, let me be a handmaiden of Holy Poverty, your bride.

S. Francis. Little Clare, are you brave enough to be a Religious? to give up all earthly happiness forever?

S. Clare. Brother Francis, whoever looks for happiness will never find it; but I think the track of Holy Poverty may bring me there at last.

The Legend of S. Francis

S. Francis. Come then, little sister, to the church, to lay down your splendours and take up your vows. When you have on your gray frock, and your golden hair is cropped, my dear old priest of S. Damian's will take you in. [*Exeunt, L.*

C<small>URTAIN</small>

ACT III

OF HIS LOVE FOR ALL CREATURES

SCENE: *A Rose Garden; above the Hedge of Roses
the Trunks and Tops of Trees.*

S. FRANCIS [*walking, sings*].

> O roses, all too red are ye,
>   Red stains your green;
> And all too great your love for me,
>   Sweet flowers, has been:
>
> For when amid your thorns I lay
>   To prick me sore,
> The ruddy branches from that day
>   Bore thorns no more.

Brother Leo!

Enter BROTHER LEO *with an axe, L.*

What are you doing, Brother?

Brother Leo. Cutting down a tree for firewood,
Brother Francis.

The Legend of S. Francis

S. Francis.   Leave a little standing, Brother Leo,
that it may shoot up again in memory of the Holy
Cross.   [*Exit* BROTHER LEO, *L.*

[*Sings.*]

> The rose-hedge lays its lengthening walls
>   Along the grass
> Till the last ray of sunlight falls,
>   Then shadows pass.
>
> Their lord they follow; with the light
>   The shadows cease.
> As dew on flowers, so lies, at night,
>   On the heart, peace.

Brother Gardener!

Enter BROTHER JUNIPER *with a spade.*

I pray you, Brother Juniper, dig not the whole of
the ground.

Brother Juniper.   But, Brother Francis, if I dig
not the hole in the ground, how shall I plant the
lettuces?

S. Francis.   I meant not that, but begged you to
leave a place untouched where the wild flowers may
come up, the scarlet anemone and the golden crocus
and the humble green creeping things.

Brother Juniper.   There are, to be sure, plenty of
creeping things and hopping things and flying things

149

to eat up all the garden, not to say the rabbits in the lettuce beds.

S. Francis.　Poor brother rabbit, we must not grudge him his share.　What are you planting, Brother?

Brother Juniper.　Little lentils, Brother, and beans, white and red, and cabbages that look like fat citizens' wives in green silk, and lettuce like their slim daughters in flounces and furbelows.

S. Francis.　I would have in every garden always some little fair plot of ground for all manner of sweet-smelling herbs and flowers, the lily of the field, aloes and cassia, the mystic rose and the lily among thorns.

[*Exit* BROTHER JUNIPER.

My little sisters the birds are all come home now and are singing their compline.　I never saw so many, I think.　My dear Brother Anthony, when the people of a certain place would not hear him, preached to the fishes, and why should the holy word be withheld from the winged creatures?　Little sisters, little sisters! [*Numbers of birds come down.*]　My little sisters the birds, ye are in all things mightily beholden to your dear Maker, and ought at all times and in all places most sweetly to praise Him. Hath He not given you inestimable liberty to come

" My little sisters, the birds."

and go on the wind, and are not ye clothed upon, yea doubly and trebly, with softness, though ye neither spin nor sew? He saved you in the ark that ye might still be glad in the world, and hath given you the sweet air, the wind and storm fulfilling His word. Ye sow not, neither do ye reap nor gather into barns, and the brooks and the hillside springs are yours to drink of; the valleys and the mountains are your abiding place, and cedar and cypress wherein to build you nests. Ah, so greatly as He hath loved you, giving you all good things, so must ye beware, little sisters, of sinful ingratitude, and ever more and more sing praises unto Him.

[*Raises his hand, they fly up.*

Enter PACIFICO, *behind, R.*

Sister moon and all my little sisters the stars are merry in the blue, and song is bubbling at my lips. [*Sings.*]

High in the shadowy cypress tree
Still broods the dove,
And my sweet lady Poverty
Is still my love.

Pacifico [*coming forward*]. God's minstrel! Brother Francis, Brother Francis, I have misdoubted you most wickedly, and when they stoned you for a madman long ago, up in Assisi, there was I by.

S. Francis. Dear Pacifico, when any man is sorry for wrong-doing, then am I glad; how great soever the wrong against me, the more happy am I.

Pacifico. But I have been a wretched idler, and unkind.

S. Francis. I am worse myself, Brother, I am worse myself than any heart but mine could dream; but when we mean to be good, then after a while we are. And this gray frock is a great remembrancer of virtue.

Pacifico. Ah, yes. In the world we forget so soon.

S. Francis. Then come out of the world.

Pacifico. May I? Dear Brother Francis, would you have me?

S. Francis [*embracing him*]. O my Brother, I would have all the world.

Pacifico. But after your sermon to-day you refused many men and women, promising to make for them a Third Order that they might live in the world and yet out of the world.

S. Francis. Not every one has the vocation of a Religious; and for such the Third Order is their place. But that you have a true vocation, I truly believe —

The Legend of S. Francis

Enter BROTHER BERNARD, *R.*

Go in now, Brother Gentleheart.

[*Exit* PACIFICO, *R.*

My Brother, you are going a long way, and it may
be you will come to see the Emperor.

Brother Bernard. I am only going for the sake
of holy obedience, Brother.

S. Francis. And for the sake of holy obedience
I am parting with you, dear Brother. I give you
as a message the thing I would have said if ever
I had come to speech of the Emperor. Pray him
first that he make a law that no one kill our
sister, the crested lark, for she is the true image
of a Religious. She is humble, and yet soars high,
ever praising more and more worthily in her earthen-
coloured coat of feathers. And pray him second that
the bailiffs of all towns and the lords of all castles
be bound on every Christmas Day to throw grain
outside the walls for our sisters the larks; and that
every man who have an ox or an ass be bound to
give of his best on that holy night to the patient
beasts that were in the stable at Bethlehem. And,
moreover, in honour of that same most glorious
night, that all poor folk, wheresoever they be, shall, by

155

the Emperor's command, be full fed by the rich, so that
that season, at least, there be no hunger anywhere.

Brother Bernard. Even so, Brother Francis, for
the devil dances in an empty stomach.

S. Francis. Now, dear Brother Bernard, the first
of all my brothers, come in and say farewell.

Brother Bernard. Ah, let me sing first, before
I go, the Canticle of the Creatures with you.

Both [*sing*].

[1] Most high, most mighty, and most gracious Lord,
To Thee all praise and honour we award,
And every blessing, for alone to Thee
Do they belong from all eternity.

Praised be my Lord for everything create :
First Brother Sun, the Light-giver, whose state
Bringing the dawn — altogether fair —
In brightness speaks of Thee, Lord, everywhere.

Praised be my Lord of radiant Sister Moon,
Crescent or waning or in plenilune ;
Of all the stars in heaven that Thou hast made
Benign in brightness that shall never fade.

Praised be my Lord of Brother Wind on high,
Air, clouds and clear, all seasons of the sky ;

[1] This was written for this arrangement, in the Hymnal, of the Russian Na-
tional hymn.

The Legend of S. Francis

Praised be my Lord of Sister Water clear,
Chaste, precious, humble, for all uses dear.

Praised be my Lord of Brother Fire by night,
Comely and joyful, masterful in might;
Of Sister Earth that cherishes and keeps
Ourselves, the grass, gay flowers, and fruits in heaps.

Praised be my Lord of them that do forgive,
And for Thy love in grief and sickness live;
Blessed are they in peace that do endure,
For them, Most Highest, Thou hast a crown secure.

Praised be my Lord, yea, praised of Sister Death,
The body's dying that awaits all breath;
Some die in sin, but those that do Thy will
The second death shall have no power to kill.

Praised be my Lord.   To Him all thanks be given,
As on the earth, so in the highest heaven.
In humbleness be service still the same,
Though none is worthy even to name His Name.

.[*Exeunt, R.*

CURTAIN

157

THE LEGEND OF S. DOROTHY

PUPPETS

THE EMPEROR OF ROME.	Armour, a purple cloak, sword, shield, helmet with crown.
THEOPHILUS, *a young nobleman.*	Court dress, gold chain.
PETERKIN, *his page.*	Clown.
A CAPTAIN.	Armour, red cloak.
S. DOROTHY, *a Christian maiden.*	Court dress of white and red.

Properties: a basket of apples and red roses, with garlands of roses dropping from it.

This is the Legend of S. Dorothy as it was told for hundreds of years, not quite truly perhaps, but not the less beautifully. Let the dress of the people be just such as in the Legend of S. Francis, and the scenery present such a city as he went about in.

The Legend of S. Dorothy

SCENE: *A Public Place.*

Enter L., THEOPHILUS *and* PETERKIN.

Theophilus. Peterkin!

Peterkin. Master!

Theophilus. What is it o'clock?

Peterkin. Dinner time, master.

Theophilus. I asked you not the time, fool, but the hour.

Peterkin. And I told you, sir, according to my means, than which no man can do more. Do you take me for the town hall, that I should wear a clock in my forehead?

Theophilus. I pray you by what means, not knowing the hour, do you tell the time?

Peterkin. Marry, sir, my stomach cries meal time, as true as a peal of bells.

Theophilus. Say like the bell over a shop door, for it jingles every five minutes.

Peterkin. Now in good faith, I hold it wiser to be dealing with good meat and wine and therewith thankful, than to be gaping at the sun and feeding on discontent.

Theophilus. Why should I be content? I have nothing to wish for.

Peterkin. Most men who wish are discontented, and with the getting of their wishes contentment comes.

Theophilus. Man's sole happiness lies in desire, and when desire is dead he might as well be all underground.

Peterkin. Where certainly there is no desiring except on the part of Goodman Worm.

Theophilus. If I drink, eat, wear fine clothes, build me a golden house, wherein am I better than the cat stealing cream, the lion springing on a goat, the peacock spreading his tail, and the bee at work upon the comb? Am I not shamed by all these? For I have neither the cunning of the cat, the strength of the lion, the beauty of the peacock, nor the science of the bee.

Peterkin. Why not be then a poet, master, and sing with more skill than the thrush, with more sense than the nightingale, and with more sweetness than the magpie?

Theophilus. Because the nightingale would outdo me in skill, the thrush in sweetness, and the pie in sense, for he asks only what he needs.

Peterkin. Then you must needs turn soldier, for he has neither skill, sweetness, nor sense.

Theophilus. Three things which I cannot do without. Neither poetry nor war is to my taste, and as for religion, with all due reverence to the immortal gods, they have less sense than a poet, less sweetness than a soldier, and less skill than a mere man who eats, drinks, and carries his clothing about.

Peterkin. I see plainly, master, that unless I find you an occupation very soon, you will walk yourself off to an asylum for lunatics and maintain them to be the only rational company. How say you, shall we go and hunt Christians?

Theophilus. I tell you, no! I'll have no hand in that matter! They are as foolish-innocent a set of folk as ever lived by bread.

Peterkin. But the Emperor takes huge delight in the new sport.

Theophilus. The Emperor is no soldier, to kill defenceless women, and no sportsman, to strike at what will neither run nor strike back. I would as lief go into the butcher's business and produce mutton and veal, as keep company with the Emperor in these days.

Enter the EMPEROR, *L.*

Emperor. By Jupiter and Apollo, 'tis a nipping day.

Peterkin. See you now, master, how wit keeps a man warm. I should have thought it was June.

Theophilus. It is seasonable weather, sire.

Emperor. Now, by Mahound, it is unseasonable if I am cold. It shall be a warm day, I say. Am I Emperor for nothing?

Theophilus. Doubtless, if your Majesty does due sacrifice to Apollo, he will at your imperial request drive his chariot near enough to the earth to relieve your Majesty's shivering fit.

Emperor. I know a trick worth two of that. Ho, guard!

Enter CAPTAIN.

Go fire me some dozen of Christians' houses in this neighbourhood, till they warm the air.

[*Exeunt* EMPEROR *and* CAPTAIN, *R.*

Theophilus. So folly finds ways to warm itself. Go home and dine, Peterkin; I have no mind to eat.

Peterkin. Nor have I, master. No, I thank the

gods I have two stout jaws to munch withal, and thirty teeth moreover.   [*Exit, L.*

Enter S. DOROTHY, *L.*

Theophilus. What goddess comes ? Too simple for Pallas, too maidenly for Venus, too —

S. Dorothy. Spare your catalogue, sir. I am but a Christian girl whose house is now a heap of ashes.

Theophilus. Lady, I had four houses — they are all yours.

S. Dorothy. I have not begged, sir.

Theophilus. Nor do I give to beggars.

S. Dorothy. I am not for sale.

Theophilus. Nor am I a slave dealer. But there are such things as friends.

S. Dorothy. Not for me among the worshippers of false gods.

Enter EMPEROR, *R.*

Emperor. Who is that, in Cupid's name ?

Theophilus. A lady, sir, to whom —

S. Dorothy. To whom you are a stranger, sir. Your Majesty, an orphan and homeless.

Emperor. I've seen your face before to-day.

S. Dorothy. Doubtless, sire, when I left my burning house just now.

Emperor. So, now I have it! We smoked the

old foxes and out pops the little white rabbit. Well [*clashing his sword against his shield*], you're done with that stuff.

S. Dorothy. Your majesty, I am a Christian.

Emperor [*same gesture*]. Now, by Mahound, you won't be long.

S. Dorothy. Always, sire. That is the only name one does not lose in death.

Emperor. That I will give you the chance of proving. Guard!

Enter CAPTAIN, *R.*

Bring her head in an hour to the palace.

Theophilus. One moment, sire. The bloodless victories of faith are the glorious ones, and it is more royal to reduce the number of unbelievers by conversion than by decapitation. The lady is not only fair but sage. Let me attempt her reason.

Emperor. By Mars, you waste your breath. In an hour's time her sacrifice or her head. I'll go make search for others. Am I not Emperor? [*Clashes his sword and strides out*, CAPTAIN *striding after*, R.]

Theophilus. Sweet lady —

S. Dorothy. Sir, you waste your breath. I go gladlier than to my bridal.

Theophilus. But, even though doubtfully, to your

"Am I not Emperor?"

The Legend of S. Dorothy

bridal, I trust. My name — you may have heard it — is Theophilus.

S. Dorothy. I have heard of you as an honourable gentleman, but one who thinks himself too wise to listen to true wisdom.

Theophilus. Dear child, you wrong the world to take your youth and beauty from it.

S. Dorothy. The truth for which I die is more beautiful than beauty's self.

Theophilus. Truth has many forms and even the foolishest gods stand in some way for goodness.

S. Dorothy. Mine is all-wise, all-good.

Theophilus. Dorothy, I will not strive to shake you there, for I know your people are immovable. But my wife could stand in no danger even from religion.

Dorothy. Your heart I know is noble; but I like better my red bridal even though the chamberlain is grim.

Theophilus. I will carry you away to an island set jewel-like in turquoise sea, where roses bloom every hour and the boughs are heavy with dropping fruits. Dear girl, the grave is dark and cold and barren, and sun is here and sweetness unchanging.

S. Dorothy. Where I go the roses never fade and the trees bear each month twelve manner of fruits.

Theophilus.   I cannot see your fruits and flowers.

S. Dorothy.   But I will send you some, if —

Theophilus.   If what?   [*With sorrowful scorn.*] Send them, and I will follow you to pluck you others.

S. Dorothy.   Then expect them.   Captain!

Enter CAPTAIN, *R.*

Theophilus.   Can you not love me, girl?

S. Dorothy.   Greatly, dear Theophilus, but not so much as martyrdom.   Remember the roses.

[*Exit, R.,* CAPTAIN *following.   Pause.*   THEOPHI-LUS *stands, his face hidden in his arm.   Here a voice or voices may sing* "*For thee, O dear, dear country,*" *or other parts of* "*The Celestial Country.*"

Enter EMPEROR, *L.*

Emperor.   Where's your girl?

Theophilus.   Your Majesty should know better than I.   By this time, I think, neither of us knows.

Emperor.   Am I not Emperor?   Is not my will the Roman law?   When I frown, do not the gods tremble on their golden seats, and the walls of heaven shake at my stride?   I will have no worship but by special orders; the gods are gods because I choose them to be.

The Legend of S. Dorothy

Enter PETERKIN *with basket.*

Peterkin. Sir, one gave me this for you: a gold-haired lad yonder, some princess' page may be, for he was pretty enough to be a girl, and proud enough to be a king's son, and sweeter-voiced than the softest singer at the Emperor's court.

Theophilus. Roses! but balmier than those I fetched me from Persian gardens; apples more golden than those of Hesper, and fragrant as spiced October. Good servant, here's my purse. Get you another master longer-lived.

Peterkin. No, faith; I'd not outlive the best of masters.

Theophilus. I will recommend you to the Emperor.

Peterkin. Since you could not recommend him to me. No, no; that were to go from flowers to frost, and by trying to climb higher, topple over into the ditch.

Theophilus. We must part, Peterkin, for my last day is almost spent, and I would not crush you in my ruin.

Peterkin. We must not part — not though it were your last penny that was spent. No more, sir, than I would offer to share your bed would I be guilty of sharing your grave, but in the ground as in the palace, I will be at your feet.

Theophilus [*taking his hand*]. Enough! Now, if you will not yet go, listen. [*To* EMPEROR.] Sire, your captain waits yonder to tell you that the blessed Dorothy has finished her martyrdom and to usher me into her presence.

Emperor. By Mahound, this is a poor joke, Theophilus. Am I not Emperor? I think I will take you at your word.

Theophilus. Your Majesty had better, for it is the last you will get from me.

Emperor [*clashing sword and shield*]. Thunder and blood!

Peterkin. That's Jupiter and Mars.

Emperor. Fool, does your master want to get his head chopped off?

Peterkin. I think that's what your Majesty wants, saving your presence.

Emperor. Is your master a Christian, fool?

Peterkin. No, your Majesty —

Theophilus. Sire, I am —

Peterkin. He's of the religion, Majesty, but it's I that am the Christian fool, for I'm not just sure what

The Legend of S. Dorothy

is the religion.   But there is no doubt that what he is, I am.   And that pretty boy yonder did not come around the corner for nothing.

Emperor.   Shall I be spoken to thus?   Shall I be so defied?   Not by Pluto!   Theophilus, if you recanted a thousand times, you should die, and the fool in your company for the more shame.

Theophilus.   I have heard that we are all brothers, and in a family there is no ill company.   Farewell, sir, I leave you to the tender mercies of your own false gods.   Come, brother, we go a-plucking roses.

Peterkin.   In February!   To think the fool should make so good an ending alongside of his master! And yet, after all, it is but a foolish ending.

Theophilus.   Some folly is wisdom, brother: that we go to prove among the red, red roses of martyrdom.

[*Exeunt, R.,* Theophilus *leading,* Emperor *striding last.*

Curtain

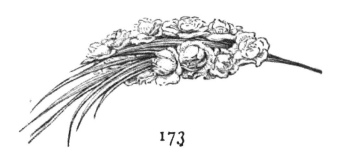

173

PANTOMIMES

SNOWFLAKE AND THE DWARFS

Snowflake and the Dwarfs

The Queen, yellow hair, pale face, white veil, after the first scene, high gold crown; fan in hand. Purple dress over pale yellow petticoat. For disguise, brown, yellow, and red peasant dress, handkerchief over her head.

Snowflake, black hair, pink cheeks, very fair face and hands. Blue dress with dark blue kirtle.

The King, very large; black hair and beard, red suit, gold crown, long sword.

The Prince, brown hair, mustache, and face; hunting suit of green; horn, sword, gold chain, and spurs.

Dwarfs, small and very square-built, with long

arms and short legs. Gray beards, brown jerkins, and boots.

Forester, black beard, hunting dress, sword.

The mirror frame is painted on the wall of the room, but the space inside of it is cut out in such a way that the painted representation of a mirror can be slipped up, from behind the scenes, as one slips off the top card from a pack, exposing to view, on the card below, a picture of the Queen in just the dress she wears. That in turn is slipped up and shows Snowflake.

The comb is of gilt paper, a high, ornamental back comb. The kirtle is golden or black, the apple of wood, painted — so the heart and tongue of the fawn. The fawn itself and the dead wolf can be bought at a toy-shop or whittled out of wood. Table and toy dishes, chair. The glass coffin is a box made of strips of glass bound together with strips of gilded cloth and has no lid — a string at one end helps to raise it. On account of the fainting scene, Snowflake's wire must be looped into a staple on top of her head instead of being solidly sunk in the head. Then she can lie out in her coffin and, as the wire is pulled up, raise herself, stand, and walk.

Scenery: (1) The Queen's house, less rich than

the palace. (2) The latter also has the mirror in the wall. (3) The forest, at a cross-road. (4) The outside of the Dwarfs' cottage with a latticed window that opens, behind which, so as to be behind any figure at it, is a plain brown curtain. (5) The inside of the cottage, showing the inside of the window, another lattice with flower-pots on the sill, a cupboard between with plates and mugs. Trees and creepers about the outside of the cottage. For Scene XIII the wings may be used from Scene III.

I

The Queen's home. Enter, L., Queen, goes to mirror, admires herself, fanning. Questions mirror about all the world, and the glass rises like a veil, showing herself, then descends again. Enter, R., King, woos her; she is first haughty, then coy, finally accepts him. Exit King, R. She again consults mirror with the same vision of herself. Reënter King, R. They embrace. Exeunt, R.

II

The palace. Enter, L., King and Queen, he tells her his daughter is returning. Exit, R. Queen consults mirror and sees herself. Enter, R., King and

Snowflake. Queen embraces her, then criticises her dress and looks. Snowflake tries to alter her appearance and manners accordingly, and exit, L. King reproaches Queen, they quarrel. Exit King, R. Queen consults mirror, sees her own image lifted like a veil in turn, and Snowflake there. Rage. Goes to wings, L., and calls Forester, orders him to kill Snowflake, calls Snowflake, L., and is very affectionate. Enter, R., King, and joins in the reconciliation. Queen sends Snowflake hunting with Forester, R.

III

The wood. Enter, R., Forester and Snowflake; he explains his business, she pleads for her life and finally moves him. Exit running, L. Enter fawn, L. Forester kills it with sword. Exit, R., with fawn.

IV

The palace. Enter, L., Queen, consults the mirror and sees herself, then instantly enter Forester, R., shows her heart and tongue. She rejoices, sends him, R., for dead wolf. Enter King, L., she weeps, telling him of Snowflake's death. Both mourn. She calls Forester, R., he brings the dead wolf and says it ate

Snowflake and the dwarfs.

Snowflake and the Dwarfs

Snowflake. After much grief, exeunt King and Forester, R. Queen hurries to mirror, rejoicing, it shows herself and then Snowflake. Rage, plans revenge. Exit, L.

V

The Dwarfs' cottage, outside. Enter, L., Snowflake much exhausted, knocks, peeps in window. Exit, L.

VI

Cottage, inside. Table laid for seven. Enter, L., Snowflake, tastes a little from each dish, falls asleep in chair. Enter, L., the seven Dwarfs, notice the table has been touched with good-natured surprise. Then one discovers her and all gather around in admiration. She wakes in terror. They reassure her, she tells her story, and they suggest her remaining as housekeeper, but warn her against the Queen. Exeunt Dwarfs, L., Snowflake, R.

VII

Dwarfs' cottage, outside. Enter, R., Queen, disguised, with pack on her back and kirtle in her hand. Knocks. Snowflake appears at the window, they talk. Queen persuades her to admit her. Snowflake leaves the window. Queen rejoices. Exit, L. Scene rises, showing inside. Enter, L., Queen and Snowflake. Queen praises her beauty, puts the kirtle on her. [They step into the wings for this.] Snowflake falls as if dead, Queen rejoices. Exit, L. Pause. Enter Dwarfs, L., mourn over Snowflake, finally take off the kirtle and she awakes. Great rejoicing and renewed warnings. Exeunt, R. and L.

VIII

Palace. Enter Queen, L., and consults mirror which shows herself. Enter King, R., unhappy and very cross. Queen soothes and comforts him, persuades him to go hunting. Exit King and Forester, R. Queen consults mirror in pride and delight; sees Snowflake. Rage and fresh plans.

IX

Dwarfs' cottage, outside. Enter Queen, R., with comb; knocks. Snowflake at window explains she cannot admit her. Queen coaxes her to come out. Enter Snowflake, L. Queen greets her, puts comb in her hair. [They step into the wings for this.]

Snowflake and the Dwarfs

Snowflake falls as if dead. Exit, R., Queen in joy. Enter, R., Dwarfs, great sorrow, finally spy comb and remove it. Snowflake recovers. Exeunt, L.

X

Palace. Enter Queen, R., consults mirror and sees herself; King returns, R., from hunting very unlucky and beats Forester. Queen soothes him till he goes off, L. She consults mirror and sees Snowflake. Faints.

XI

Dwarfs' cottage, outside. Enter Queen, triumphant, in a third disguise. Knocks. Snowflake at window will not let her in. Queen offers apple, tasting it herself. Exit, R. Scene rises, shows inside of cottage: Snowflake eyes the apple, finally eats and dies. Enter, L., Dwarfs, in ever growing distress as they cannot revive her. Bring on glass coffin and lay her therein, weeping bitterly.

XII

Palace. Enter, L., Queen, consults mirror and is well satisfied. Enter, R., King mournful. She

taunts him with Snowflake's death. He beats her
and exit, R. Queen again goes to mirror and sees
only herself.

XIII

Dwarfs' cottage, outside. The glass coffin, with
Snowflake in it, at the R., a Dwarf beside it. Trees
and creepers about the cottage much thicker and
taller than before. [Extra painted parts being stuck
on them.] Enter, L., Prince, asks his way, then a
drink. Exit Dwarf, L., Prince sees Snowflake, falls in
love; reënter Dwarf, L., with cup. Prince begs for
her. Enter the other six Dwarfs, R. Prince begs
so earnestly that, though they refuse his money indig-
nantly, they finally give her to him, weeping. They
start to lift the coffin, two at each end. It falls with a
jar, Snowflake stirs, moves, sits up, rises, and steps out
amid the joy of all. Embraces all the Dwarfs, then
sees the Prince and is frightened; they present him,
he woos and finally wins her. After tender farewells,
exeunt Prince and Snowflake, R., happy, Dwarfs, L.,
weeping.

XIV

Palace. Enter, L., Queen, hair powdered, white
veil, consults mirror and is haughty and vain seeing

Snowflake and the Dwarfs

herself. Enter, R., King, hair and beard powdered, old, feeble, unhappy, rebukes her vanity; they quarrel, he beats her, then cries feebly and makes up. She goes back to mirror and is thunderstruck by seeing Snowflake's image. Calls King and both are unable to understand. Exit Queen, L. Enter, R., Forester. King tells him the situation, he confesses and exit, R. Enter, R., Snowflake and Prince, and embrace the King. Enter, L., Queen. King reproaches and kills her. General rejoicing.

MOTHER HUBBARD AND HER DOG

.

Mother Hubbard and her Dog

The scenery should be painted on cloth, *e.g.* paper muslin, and fastened to rollers arranged to roll up and let down. For instance, the first scene shows Mother Hubbard's house; when she goes out there drops over this, in full sight of the audience, a view of the outside of the house, past which she goes with different movement of eagerness, apprehension, or distress in the successive scenes. When she has gone off, the butcher's shop is dropped over it while she buys her meat, then that is rolled up; she hurries home, the house is rolled up in turn, and she enters on her room. Sometimes the curtain must be drawn between scenes, as when the dog is dead.

Comedies and Legends for Marionettes

Mother Hubbard's house might be copied from Shakespeare's at Stratford, — brown, with beams a darker brown. Blue sky above, no smoke from chimney.

Indoors, a kitchen wainscoted halfway up brown, light brown above. R., a tall chimneypiece with very small fire. L., the double doors of a cupboard, equally tall, which are made to open by strings attached to the outer edge of each door, and are hinged with very thin, tough paper: shelves, with a jug and plate painted in slight perspective. On the chimney a chamber candlestick, and above it a picture.

The market is two or three booths or small shops with the emblematic signs over the entrance. There may be several of these sets to embrace the list of trades, or different signs may be stuck in the same space with cobbler's wax. The tradesmen stand before their doors and run off to fetch their goods: there is much chaffering, and the tradesmen go out with Mother Hubbard carrying her purchases. She reappears on the homeward way with the articles stuck to her hand as usual with cobbler's wax.

Mother Hubbard is dressed in a red or brown frock made like the Mother Hubbard wrappers that take their name from her; she wears a mob cap and spectacles, and carries a cane in her left hand, a long purse or bag in her right when she goes to market.

The Baker, small; white apron and floury black trousers, square cap. Sign: yellow pretzel on a blue ground.

The Joiner, thin; long, narrow, brown apron, paper cap. Sign: white skull on black ground.

The Vintner, fat; dull red smock frock. Sign: a green bush.

The Hatter, very large; gray clothes. Sign: a Rough Rider's hat.

The Barber, fat and small; white apron. Sign: a striped pole.

The Fruiterer, dressed as a peasant; blue smock, round, soft hat. Sign: a bunch of grapes.

The Tailor, very small and thin; black clothes. Sign: a pair of shears, black on a yellow ground.

The Cobbler, small, fat, and jolly; leathern apron, very dirty face and hands. Sign: a large awl.

The Hosier, very tall and thin; dressed in yellow. Sign: a green stocking.

The Dog can be bought at any toy-shop — the white, fluffy kind like a poodle is best. If one cannot be found with the hind legs jointed, take these off and pivot them on a wire, the ends of which are quite hidden in the thick curly hair. His lower jaw should work also. His wire is in the middle of his back, fastened to the ring of a screw-eye.

The Cat and the Goat are similar figures with less need of joints.

Other properties are: loaf of bread, three coffins, red cocked hat, brown curled wig like a barrister's, two other wigs of any sort, a bunch of grapes, a flute, a blue coat with large brass buttons, red shoes, a newspaper, a bottle of wine, red stockings, a table and toy dishes, two chairs.

I

Kitchen. Enter Dog sniffing about, gradually whimpers, finally howls. Enter Mother Hubbard, L., a rather decrepit but very excitable old lady, tries to make out the trouble, goes to fire and then to wings. He sits up and begs, she finally realizes, pets and promises him a good dinner, opens cupboard door. Despair! Exit Mother Hubbard, R., Dog following her crestfallen.

II

Outside. Enter Mother Hubbard, R., in great excitement pausing to wave the Dog back. Returns

to R. entrance once or twice to make sure he is safe;
exit, L.

Baker's.   Enter Mother Hubbard, R.   Elaborate
explanation, much pacing up and down till Baker
returns, L., with loaf.   She pays instantly.   Exeunt,
R.   [Curtain falls a moment.]

Kitchen.   Dog stretched out on the hearth.   Enter,
R., Mother Hubbard bursts into tears, after much
grief, exit, R.   Dog jumps up and exit, L.

III

Outside.   She goes slowly, pausing to weep.

Joiner's.   Conversation much interrupted by her
grief.   Joiner weeps sympathetically.   Exit Joiner,
L., and returns with coffin which is rejected because
too small.   Another is too large, and third is right.
Exeunt together.

Outside.   She pauses often before summoning
courage to enter the house.

Kitchen.   Empty.   Enter Mother Hubbard, amazed,
searches everywhere; finally enter, L., Dog wagging
his lower jaw, leaping and twisting.   She embraces
him and strokes his head, is struck with an idea
about his head, exit.

IV

Outside. In her gladness stops to look back and rejoice.

Hatter's. Hastily takes the first hat that offers.

Outside. Still overcome with emotion.

Kitchen. Enter Dog with Cat and a large spoon, she finally escapes and exit, L., Dog following. Enter Mother Hubbard, R., and crosses stage with hat. Enter Dog with hat on, L., followed by Mother Hubbard. It is much too large. Exit Mother Hubbard.

V

Outside. Vexed with her own stupidity. Goes back to R. entrance and calls the Dog on, looks at him again, sends him off, exit, L.

Barber's. He brings on different sorts of wigs. She selects one.

Outside. Dog runs out to meet her.

Kitchen. Dog dances in on his hind legs, wearing the wig and preceding Mother Hubbard. They dance a minuet together. [Curtain for a moment.]

Mother Hubbard.

Mother Hubbard and her Dog

VI

Fruiterer's. She calls for grapes, rejecting apples, but argues over the price a long time, thinking the dealer extortionate.

Outside. She stops to eat some grapes.

Kitchen. As she enters, R., Dog enters, L., on his hind legs, holding flute to his mouth with his fore paws. She listens with rapture, then strokes his back and goes to the fire. Exit with him.

VII

Outside. She is leading him.

Tailor's. Tailor takes the Dog's measure, then Dog runs off. She waits impatiently, calling the tailor and scolding him twice before she gets the coat.

Outside. Pauses and listens in wonder to the sounds from within.

Kitchen. Enter Dog on Goat, rides him round. Enter Mother Hubbard, amazed and angry. Chases both out. Mother Hubbard perplexed a long time. Exit, R.

VIII

Still wondering what to do, Mother Hubbard stumbles on a stone and has an inspiration.

CPSIA information can be obtained
at www.ICGtesting.com
Printed in the USA
BVHW041355110219
539955BV00015B/519/P